One True God
80 devotions

A 180-DEGREE LIFE-CHANGING 80-DAY
DEVOTIONAL WRITTEN BY PEOPLE LIKE YOU

G4C
publications

2020 by Jessica Lippe and the authors listed on their respective page(s)

All rights reserved. This book or any portion thereof may not be reproduced or used in any manner whatsoever without the express written permission of the publisher except for the use of brief quotations in a book review

Scriptures marked AMP are taken from the AMPLIFIED BIBLE (AMP): Scripture taken from the AMPLIFIED® BIBLE, Copyright © 1954, 1958, 1962, 1964, 1965, 1987 by the Lockman Foundation Used by Permission. (www.Lockman.org)

Scriptures marked BSB are taken from the Berean Study Bible (BSB) Copyright ©2016, 2018 by Bible Hub Used by Permission. All Rights Reserved Worldwide.

Scriptures marked CSB have been taken from the Christian Standard Bible®, Copyright © 2017 by Holman Bible Publishers. Used by permission. Christian Standard Bible® and CSB® are federally registered trademarks of Holman Bible Publishers.

Scriptures marked ESV are taken from the THE HOLY BIBLE, ENGLISH STANDARD VERSION (ESV): Scriptures taken from THE HOLY BIBLE, ENGLISH STANDARD VERSION ® Copyright© 2001 by Crossway, a publishing ministry of Good News Publishers. Used by permission.

Scriptures marked HCSB are taken from the HOLMAN CHRISTIAN STANDARD BIBLE (HCSB): Scripture taken from the HOLMAN CHRISTIAN STANDARD BIBLE, copyright© 1999, 2000, 2002, 2003 by Holman Bible Publishers, Nashville Tennessee. All rights reserved.

Scriptures marked NASB are taken from the NEW AMERICAN STANDARD BIBLE®, Copyright © 1960,1962,1963,1968,1971,1972,1973,1975,1977,1995 by The Lockman Foundation. Used by permission.

Scriptures marked NIV are taken from the NEW INTERNATIONAL VERSION (NIV): Scripture taken from THE HOLY BIBLE, NEW INTERNATIONAL VERSION ®. Copyright© 1973, 1978, 1984, 2011 by Biblica, Inc.™. Used by permission of Zondervan

Scriptures marked NLT are taken from the HOLY BIBLE, NEW LIVING TRANSLATION (NLT): Scriptures taken from the HOLY BIBLE, NEW LIVING TRANSLATION, Copyright© 1996, 2004, 2007 by Tyndale House Foundation. Used by permission of Tyndale House Publishers, Inc., Carol Stream, Illinois 60188. All rights reserved. Used by permission.

Scriptures marked NKJV are taken from the NEW KING JAMES VERSION (NKJV): Scripture taken from the NEW KING JAMES VERSION®. Copyright© 1982 by Thomas Nelson, Inc. Used by permission. All rights reserved.

Scripture quotations marked TPT are from The Passion Translation®. Copyright © 2017, 2018 by Passion & Fire Ministries, Inc. Used by permission. All rights reserved. ThePassionTranslation.com.

First Printing, 2020

G4C Publications
Girlz4Christ.org

Introduction

Picture for a moment what your life would be like if everything was different. And by different, I mean that nothing at all was the same as your current life. We're talking a complete one-eighty. If you're tall, you'd be short. If you're the oldest of your siblings, suddenly you'd be the youngest in the lineup. You'd live on the opposite side of the world. (Look at a globe try to find out exactly where you'd be living- it might be interesting!)

It's hard to think of every aspect of your life that could be turned upside-down. We can't even begin to imagine how it would all feel because we're so used to living a certain unique lifestyle. But is that a good thing or a bad thing?

A lot of your life right now is exactly where God wants you to be. He created you for a specific purpose, and your individual upbringing, experiences, and place could be preparing you for the calling that the Lord has in store for you. But have you ever felt like God was tugging on your heart? That there's a greater plan, and you need to respond in some way?

Or maybe you're reading about this God stuff with some skepticism. Maybe you're walking opposite from the way of the Lord, but is a 180-degree life turn what you really need?

We all have things we want to improve in our lives. You might want to be smarter, richer, prettier, more athletic, and the list goes on. But have you ever asked what God wants to improve in your life?

The biggest one-eighty God wants us to make is to repent from sin. *Repent* literally means making a 180-turn. He wants us living in a way so different from our former sinful selves that it's countercultural. That's why this book is titled **One True God, 80 Devotions**, as a reminder that there is only one God, who is calling us to live a one-eighty life. Of course, it's partly named that because this is an 80-day devotional.

God not only wants us to not live in sin, but to live in Christ. He loves us so much that we get to have a personal relationship with the Lord. You probably have several other important relationships in your life, like with relatives or friends. Think of one of these people that you have a good relationship with. Now what would happen if you didn't talk to them, didn't read the messages they sent you, didn't take advantage of the amazing opportunities they offered you, and barely knew them at all? It would be hard to maintain a good relationship if you ignored them except for the times when you wanted something. Unfortunately, a lot of people treat our special relationship with God just like that.

In order to grow in your walk with Christ, you need to work on your relationship. Learn more about God. Have conversations (that's called prayer). Read the letters God has given you (those are bound together in a book called the Bible). If you feel like your relationship with God is weakening instead of growing stronger, perhaps it's time to take a one-eighty in your Christian walk as well.

That's what this book is for. These short daily readings will only take you a few minutes tops, but can jumpstart the time you spend with God in a powerful way. Each day includes a passage straight from the Bible, a relevant message explaining why that Biblical truth is important, and an action that you can personally do to apply God's Word to your own life. Here are a few tips to make the most of this devotional:

- Decide on a time of day to do your devotions. A lot of people find it habitual to do this first thing in the morning, but others enjoy it as part of their bedtime routine. Or, instead of a specific time, you could schedule devotions before or after a certain activity. Maybe you could read on the bus ride home or while sitting at the dinner table.
- Don't be in a rush. Give yourself more time than just what's needed to read. You can spend any extra time re-reading parts you want to understand better, reading the Bible to get a better context of the daily verse, and praying about what you just read.
- If something comes up and you do end up missing a day, don't give up! You could double up on devos the next day, but adding an extra day to your reading plan tends to have a better long-term effect.
- This devotional can last you much longer than 80 days. Feel free to go back and repeat certain devos that had an impact on you. Read through it slower with a Bible study group. Use it as inspiration to write your own devos!

An especially exciting thing about this book is that it was written by 27 different guys and girls from all over the world. You might find an author that you particularly relate to, or one that can provide a new perspective that you never thought of before. So you may notice that each day's devotion has a different voice, but all of them point to the one true God.

To Nathan,

I pray this book helps you live out your love for God more and more. Happy Reading! :)

Thank you for your friendship and support

Sophie

August 2020

Day One

Fixing our eyes on Jesus, the pioneer and perfecter of faith. For the joy set before him he endured the cross, scorning its shame, and sat down at the right hand of the throne of God. Hebrews 12:2-3 (NIV)

Have you ever felt like giving up on a dream, project, or goal…just before you finally grasped it? Anything worthwhile is something worth fighting for—but sometimes we lose sight of the finish line, get sidetracked along the way, or convince ourselves that our goal just isn't "worth it". Sometimes this even happens in our walk with God—the enemy sneaks in and makes us question if we're on the right track. And, when that happens, sometimes all we need is an extra bit of perseverance.

Perseverance isn't easy to come by—we have to dig deep for it. Dig into ourselves? No. Dig into Christ and His word. When we ask God for the strength and fortitude to press on through persecution and temptation, He will give us all that we need. It might feel like our perseverance tank is empty, but God is ready and waiting to fill it. And, with His help, we can all cross the finish line.

Action If you've been feeling "stuck" in your walk with the Lord, go to Him today and ask Him to refill you with a love for Him, a desire to do His will, and enough perseverance to see you through the end of the race called life.

Taylor Bennett

Day Two

For I am sure that neither death nor life, nor angels nor rulers, nor things present nor things to come, nor powers, nor height nor depth, nor anything else in all creation, will be able to separate us from the love of God in Christ Jesus our Lord. Romans 8:38-39 (ESV)

Nothing can separate us from the love God has for us.

How amazing to know these words can bring us peace and be a powerful reminder that we can overcome. This deserves repeating. Nothing – not our fears, not our insecurities, not the actions of others, not our families, not our failures, not our "unworthiness," not even death – can truly separate us from the love of God. This means we are never without hope. Our situation is never too bad, too far gone, too bleak, too ugly, or too messy for God and His amazing grace.

The enemy and past/present human pain can tempt us to keep our hearts walled off, closed up, or shut down in efforts to protect ourselves. Satan and all evil are constantly speaking lies to us all, so we need to be on guard and surround ourselves with truth.

Don't believe the lies that you aren't worthy, that this type of love isn't real, or that God doesn't care about your situation. God calls us out of this fear, away from these lies, and into faith. It's only in receiving God's gifts of love and grace (and this is a repeated process) that true and lasting healing, unshakeable love, and transformation enters into our life.

Thanks to this scripture, even when we can't feel it or are caught in a moment of unbelief, we can be sure that God's love is always there. The most wonderful truth we can know is that God's love is constant…yesterday, today, and forever!

Action What truth has God opened your eyes to see? Take a moment to reflect; writing down any of your thoughts, questions, and prayers in response.

Bethany Hamilton

Day Three

There is salvation in no one else! God has given no other name under heaven by which we must be saved. Acts 4:12 (NLT)

I carried firewood down to my family's firepit. I was about to start a fire and get ready for our cookout. As I dropped the logs into the pit, something wriggled in the ashes. Upon closer inspection, I found a little lizard!

The ash-covered lizard had easily made his way into the firepit, but because of the slick metal sides, he was unable to crawl out on his own. Knowing he would die a brutal death if he was in there when the fire started, I first tried to get him out. I reached my hand down to help him, but he struggled and ran away in fear. All his attempts to get out on his own just ended with him getting covered in more ashes. It took a while, but eventually, he did allow me to pick him out and take him to a better place, where he was safe from the upcoming fire.

As I later roasted my dinner over the flames, I couldn't stop thinking about how that little lizard was so much like all of us. We've all fallen into a pit of sin that we couldn't get out of on our own. Our struggle has often led us to be covered in even more sin. We have heard of this Greater Power who can pull us out of the ashes. But to some of us, that's a scary thought! And others would rather continue rolling in the ashes of sin than be humble enough to accept guidance and help. But putting our trust in God is the only way we'll ever be able to experience freedom.

Action If you haven't yet put your trust in God, there is no better time than today. Once you've made that commitment to have the Lord lead your life, continue to seek God. He is the only one who can see the full picture of your life, the future, and the world. So it only makes sense to put your faith in God for everything! Pray and ask the Lord to guide your next steps.

Jessica Lippe

Day Four

For God has not given us a spirit of fear, But of power and of love and of a sound mind. 2 Timothy 1:7 (NKJV)

Have you ever been afraid? I know that I have. Life can be scary sometimes, and the world can feel overwhelming at times. We have life choices to make… school, careers, spouses… as well as living in a fallen world with crime and hate. It can become easy to go to fear as our default reaction.

But God has a much better way. The Bible tells us that He has not given us a spirit of fear. He doesn't want you to be afraid of the future, and certainly not afraid of Him. He loves you and cares about you! That is why He does give us power, love, and a sound mind. Power to walk in victory in this world. Love to reach out to others, our friends and families. A sound mind to have wisdom to know Him, and learn His heart. He has given us the Holy Spirit to teach us along the way, so the world won't seem so scary after all.

Action What is something that you have always wanted to do, but were afraid to try? Join a new club, try out for a new sport, learn a new language? Find something you are excited about doing, then pray and ask the Lord to give you the power, love, and sound mind to do so. Ask Him for courage and boldness!

Lori Findlaytor

Day Five

Wealth gained hastily will dwindle, but whoever gathers little by little will increase it. Proverbs 13:11 (ESV)

There are no shortcuts to success.

As a teen author and entrepreneur, I often find myself jealous of those who seem to find 'instant success'. Those who sign a big book deal or win an award. They put in the effort and time all then all of a sudden, they're there. Sometimes I find myself wanting to get there, wherever 'there' is. I want my big break. I want to make it.

But the truth is, dreams don't come true overnight or all of a sudden. God doesn't want us to step into our wealth or success until we're ready for it, he doesn't want 'big breaks' he wants slow, steady, and healthy progress. We raise ourselves higher and accomplish our goals little by little, step by step through small, everyday actions. The 'hasty' shortcuts don't last, but the steady progress sticks with you. As the old saying goes, 'slow and steady wins the race.'

Action Do you have some big goals you want to achieve? Instead of rushing to achieve them, embrace the journey. Break the goal down into small action steps that you can achieve 'little by little' every day.

Millie Florence

Day Six

And I am sure of this, that he who began a good work in you will bring it to completion at the day of Jesus Christ. Philippians 1:6 (ESV)

Growing up, I had big dreams and a deep passion for Christ. I was so excited to serve him, and I wanted to inspire other people my age to live for God.

At that time, I had no idea that I'd later go through intense depression, among other struggles, that made me lose sight of who I was in Christ. I didn't see myself as he saw me; I saw myself as a failure who wasn't living for Jesus like I should have been. It seemed as if I had irreparably "messed up" God's plan for my life.

What the Lord has taught me coming out the other side of depression, even though I still struggle sometimes, (and we all struggle with things) is that he has a plan for me through the dark times in my life and that he's not finished with me yet. No matter what you've done or what you've gone through, God is still calling you to himself. He wants to use your life and your testimony for his glory. He can use the things you go through to help you relate to others who have been through similar situations and encourage them. And he can use every circumstance in your life to strengthen your faith and help you grow in your relationship with him. God's not finished with you!

Action Do what James 4:8 (ESV) says: "Draw near to God, and he will draw near to you." Pour out your heart to your heavenly father. He is with you through your struggles! He hasn't given up on you.

Talia Ward

Day Seven

Better is one day in your courts than a thousand elsewhere; I would rather be a doorkeeper in the house of my God than dwell in the tents of the wicked. Psalm 84:10 (NIV)

When I think about the most beautiful place I have ever experienced, my mind drifts to Mexico. If I close my eyes, I can see the white beaches, swaying palm trees, and green-covered hills. I can feel the warmth of sunshine on my skin and the sand between my toes. I can taste the saltwater and hear the gently crashing ocean waves. On this gray, dreary day in Northwest Ohio, that sure sounds good right now!

Amazingly, the Bible tells us there is an even better place to be- in the presence of God. The writer of the above verse knew that spending 1,000 days in the most amazing place on earth could not compare to the loveliness of being with the King of the Universe. How can this be?

When we come before God with open hearts in prayer and praise, we experience the richness of His infinite love. Truly, there is no place more beautiful than when we enter into the courts of our God. May this be our heart's deepest desire.

Action Ask God to make Him the desire of your heart. Spend 2-3 minutes in silent prayer reflecting on His love and goodness.

Nicole Byrum

Day Eight

I can do all this through him who strengthens me. Philippians 4:13 (NIV)

When it comes to life, I have learned that it is not always easy. We go through unexpected trials that help us grow as a person. I could have never conquered the trials in my life without three things: my family, the Bible, and, most importantly, the Lord.

You see, without God, it is more difficult to overcome life challenges. During the most difficult times, I have picked up my Bible and a verse would come up and it had to do with my life experience. The Lord brings us comfort that nobody else can bring us.

Big things for us are nothing that God can't handle. What we see as something that we can't do, God says, "I can." That is why it is important to trust in God and have faith no matter what. He has a plan for you, and whatever it is, you have to say, "God, my future is in your hands and you have special plans beyond my understanding." You are an overcomer, you can do this.

Action Pray and read the Bible daily. When you pray and read the scriptures it makes such a difference and by doing this it really changes your life. It does not matter what time of day it is as you're walking you can pray and even if you're not going through trials you can simply give thanks to God for everything and all the blessings that have come upon your life. Instead of watching that TV first, take time for a devotional.

Tiara Cirino

Day Nine

Declare his glory among the nations, his marvelous deeds among all peoples. 1 Chronicles 16:24 (NIV)

How do you use social media?

I used to put videos on YouTube and I remember reading this verse in the Bible one day and being like 'yes, this is what my YouTube channel is for!' Admittedly, I don't post on YouTube anymore. But I still think social media is a great way to shout about God, His glory, and His deeds, across millions of people.

My relationship with Instagram is very much a love-hate relationship. I hate how much time I spend looking at stuff on there, but I love being able to share positive posts, prayers and Bible verses that will get seen by non-Christian friends and family members. I pray that somehow, through the things I post, these people are being drawn nearer to God.

How do you use your social media accounts? What sort of things do you post? If someone looked at your feed would they know you love Jesus?

Action Choose your own action today: Either spend the entire day without social media and use your time to focus on God instead, or post something on your account that will draw others to God.

Sophie Spree

Day Ten

If this be so, our God whom we serve is able to deliver us from the burning fiery furnace, and he will deliver us out of your hand, O king. But if not, be it known to you, O king, that we will not serve your gods or worship the golden image that you have set up. Daniel 3:17-18 (ESV)

In the book of Daniel, Shadrach, Meshach, and Abednego are accused of not bowing down to King Nebuchadnezzar and his gold. In an era of brazen calves and idolatry, these actions are countercultural and directly disobey Nebuchadnezzar's command (Daniel 3:5-6, ESV).

At this moment, I smell fire. The heat profusely boiling as the flicks of light eat up the flames. My faith quivers for the endurance of these men to follow Jesus. But for us, we know the end of the story. Jesus walked into the fire with them, and when they walked out, not a smell, burn, or an ounce of ashes reflected their luminous skin, yet the heart of God who was with them did.

Perhaps you're facing a fire of your own, and though it may be less literal, be encouraged. Jesus will ask you to walk through difficulties of suffering, but He will never ask you to do so alone. He not only goes into the inferno with us, but He lives within us when we make it out stronger than when we first entered.

Action Lord, let faith inspire us to walk through our fires with confidence, knowing that even if you don't deliver us, we will stay dedicated to your purpose for our lives.

Amber Ginter

Day Eleven

A friend loves at all times, and a brother is born for a time of adversity.
Proverbs 17:17 (NIV)

Since I was young, my closest friends were guys. We've hung out, watched Marvel movies, and laughed over stupid things. I didn't realize that they would be some of the most reliable people in my life.

For a long time, I struggled socially with cues and social skills. Being autistic, I was bullied in elementary and middle school and became self-critical in high school and college. Yet, even with my flaws, hurts, and constant "therapy sessions," they love and accept me. On the days where I believed that I was bringing them down with my negativity, they encouraged me and stood by me when I needed them most. One of them said it best one day: "Succeeding together feels better than failing alone."

I still think about that to this day and am thankful for the loyalty they've shown me for the past several years. This Proverb, when I read it, reminds me of what he had said to me. It reminds me that while my friends have been loyal to me, God has been so much more. He has never left me and loves me as His creation, and I truly couldn't ask for more.

Action Think back on the times where your friends have been supportive and helped you through a tough time. Be sure to thank them for being there for you when you needed them the most, and return the favor by being there for them when they need you the most.

Annika Asplund

Day Twelve

Do not conform to the pattern of this world, but be transformed by the renewing of your mind. Then you will be able to test and approve what God's will is- His good, pleasing, and perfect will. Romans 12:2 (NIV)

We all want to be a part of something special, something bigger than ourselves, a community. We all want to believe we make a difference by being part of this world. But honestly, sometimes the ways of this world are not the best examples for us to follow.

Scripture tells us not to be like the world, not to behave or follow the culture or standards of the world- like sex, drinking, and drugs to be cool. Paul tells us in Romans that we need to renew our mind, get a new mindset and new understanding to know what the will of God is. We are taught to see and think about our lives and our choices from God's point of view.

We know that God always has our best interest at heart. His ways are always loving and faithful. He is patient and kind to those who call on Him. If you want to know what God's plan and purpose is for your life, then you have to "be transformed by the renewing of your mind" and ask Him to show you His perspective.

Action Take a few minutes today to think about where your thoughts lead you. What do you spend your time thinking about? Ask God to show you where your thoughts are different than His thoughts. Then ask Him to renew your mind and give you His thoughts and understanding.

Lori Findlaytor

Day Thirteen

Having been deeply rooted [in Him] and now being continually built up in Him and [becoming increasingly more] established in your faith, just as you were taught, and overflowing in it with gratitude. Colossians 2:7 (AMP)

Whatever you feed is what will grow. You can choose to feed fear, or greed, or bitterness. But I hope you instead choose to feed your faith. When your faith is fed regularly, it builds the stamina to stand against whatever life throws at you.

When your heart is filled with the right and positive information, your faith is stirred to perform effectively. The only infallible information is the word of God.

Romans 10:17 explains that faith comes by hearing and hearing by the word of God. In other words, faith grows when the right word is heard.

Feed your faith through the word of God, the word makes you see the possibilities in God, not the impossibilities inherent in you.

Faith is not passive. "You see his faith and his actions worked together, his actions made his faith complete" (James 2:22, NLT).

A life built on faith is a life built on solid rock.

Action What are you feeding in your life? Think about the time you designate toward your thoughts, your relationships, and your work. How much are you feeding those areas in comparison with your faith?

Emmanuel Olapade

Day Fourteen

God is our refuge and strength, an ever-present help in trouble. Therefore we will not fear, though the earth give way and the mountains fall into the heart of the sea Psalm 46:1-2 (NIV)

My foot was on the brakes as I paused to determine how I was going to maneuver out of the parking lot. I looked back and saw a car's brake lights blink on. The car crept backward heading straight into me. I panicked but remained frozen with my foot still on the brakes. Then I heard a "bang!"

No damage to my truck, but the other vehicle had a hole in the bumper…

Two hours of tears, a growing headache, a growling stomach, and the police had yet to inform me of their ETA.

I couldn't leave. I didn't want to be ticketed for a hit and run. I was surrounded by a siege of stress.

That's when it hit me. I failed to seek God's ever-present help in trouble.

Seeking God's strength in sieges of stress changes our thoughts which changes our conversations. We will be able to shift from a point of fear into a place of peace.

After turning to God and surrendering my situation, I saw the smallness of it all and was able to wait with peace. With His strength, our sieges of stress don't have to succumb to the end of us.

Action Think of a time you sought the Lord after a period of stress. Journal about how He redeemed you, and how you were able to approach the situation with a different angle.

Britney Froese

Day Fifteen

The LORD will fight for you; you need only to be still. Exodus 14:14 (NIV)

I interpret this verse as needing to be still, not fighting against God or our enemies, because God will defeat our enemies in His time using His way. I don't see it as a passive and lazy not-doing-anything kind of still, but a "Be still, and know that I am God;" (Psalm 46:10 NIV) kind of still. I think it is a reverent stillness, out of awe.

God promises to protect His own from all that will not end up good for them. '"Because he loves me," says the LORD, "I will rescue him; I will protect him, for he acknowledges my name."' – Psalm 91:14 (NIV)

This doesn't mean trouble will never come our way – it means that the Lord will help us during trials, and circumstances will never be able to overcome us. This verse, much like the Exodus one, does not mean we can sit back, relax, and do nothing our whole lives. Rather, it means, as Paul writes, 'in all these things we are more than conquerors through him who loved us.' – Romans 8:37 (NIV)

Action When we worship and pray, things happen. Play some worship music and turn up the volume; pray out loud, talking to God about battles you feel that you are facing. Ask Him to fight for you.

Sophie Spree

Day Sixteen

If you claim to be religious but don't control your tongue, you are just fooling yourself, and your religion is worthless. James 1:26 (NIV)

I have been in different situations where someone came to me to vent about an issue but ended up slandering the person. Most of the time, I am expected to say something so that she doesn't feel like she's doing all the talking. In a bid to please, I say things I'm not supposed to about the other person that I regret later. I also often feel like a hypocrite whenever I eventually get to chat with the person whose name I had soiled. I know I can never take back what I had said or defend myself if the issue blows up.

The one thing I always try to avoid is being called upon to defend something I said that was misunderstood or something I never said. Believe it or not, people have a way of shifting the blame on you and making you look like the bad egg.

So I asked the Holy Spirit for help and He helped me navigate the situation. When someone older comes to complain about what someone else has done, I just smile and say, ' it is well'. When someone my age or younger than me has a complaint against a person, I politely change the conversation or excuse myself. Even if what the person is telling me is legit, it is my responsibility to bridle my tongue. Scripture says, "My dear brothers and sisters, be quick to listen, slow to speak, and slow to get angry." James 1:19 NIV

You don't need to feel stuck or alone. You have God's grace through the Holy Spirit to help you withstand any temptation. He alone can do the heavy lifting and if you ever need to say anything about that issue He will put the right words in your mouth.

Action Make a decision today to cut off from any relationship that leaves you feeling guilty after each conversation. You are not a dumping ground.

Hannah Udobia

Day Seventeen

Rejoice always, pray continually, give thanks in all circumstances; for this is God's will for you in Christ Jesus. 1 Thessalonians 5:16-18 (NIV)

I don't know about you, but I am one of those people who wants to do a million different things in life and can't settle on one career or passion to pursue. I have asked myself countless times through high school and college, "Is this what I really want to do? Will this give me purpose in life? Is this God's will for me?"

It is so easy to get hung up on a decision because you are not sure what the best option is or what God wants for your life. Through my experiences, I have learned (and am still learning!) that God's will does not have to be mysterious. Look at what this verse tells us: God's will is for us to rejoice, pray, and give thanks in all circumstances. I can do that no matter what career I have, no matter where I live, and no matter what situation I find myself in.

God has given each of you talents and abilities; use those to glorify Him, and you will be right where God wants you to be.

Action Do you struggle to know what God wants you to do? Take a minute and write down the things that excite you and the things you are good at. Now write down ways you can glorify God in those endeavors. Pray and ask God to help you to rejoice, pray, and give thanks in whatever situation He has you in right now.

Annie Joransen

Day Eighteen

The King will reply, 'Truly I tell you, whatever you did for one of the least of these brothers and sisters of mine, you did for me. Matthew 25:40 (NIV)

To most people, a squeegee is something you use at the gas station to clean the bug guts off your car windows. But when I look at a squeegee, I see more than a useful tool- I see a reminder that I serve Jesus by serving others.

When I was in high school, I went on a mission trip to Toronto, Canada. Throughout the week, we gave away sandwiches and bottles of water to the homeless living on the city streets. However, we also served the teenagers known as "squeegee kids." They were given this nickname because they cleaned the windshields of the cars stopped in traffic in exchange for a little money. To help them out, we squeegeed the windows in their place so they could have a much-needed break. They greatly appreciated the rest as well as the money we were able to earn for them.

In light of the above verse, we didn't just give sandwiches and water to the homeless. We gave them to Jesus. And all those car windows we cleaned? We did that for Jesus too. Indeed, we show love to our Savior when we serve the least of these.

Action Who in your everyday life would you consider to be "the least of these?" Write down one way you can show them love by serving them- then do it!

Nicole Byrum

Day Nineteen

Set your mind on things above, Not on things on the earth. Colossians 3:2 (NKJV)

What grabs your attention? What fills your thoughts? What occupies your time?

In today's fast-paced, instant-gratification world, there are so many things competing for your focus. Family, friends, school, work, and so much more. There are also the challenges of current events, social issues, people hurting, politics, and uncertainty all around us. It is easy to lose our peace, but we don't have to.

When Jesus and His disciples were on the sea, a great storm came up. The disciples were afraid. Jesus, who was asleep in the boat, woke up and calmed the sea, winds, and the waves with just His words. He then asked the disciples, "Why are you so fearful? How is it that you have no faith?" (Mark 4:40)

When we look at the difficult circumstances around us in our lives, we often take our eyes off of Jesus. Our minds can be filled with worry and doubt. That is why we are taught to set our mind (our affection and our thoughts) on the things above, like Jesus' love and mercy.

Action Pray that the Lord would help you to focus more on Him. Ask Him in times of fear and frustration to calm the "storm" and turn your thoughts and mind to the things above.

Lori Findlaytor

Day Twenty

If anyone would come after me, let him deny himself and take up his cross daily and follow me. Luke 9:23 (ESV)

Fake. Unfortunately, people describe Christians this way. They quickly highlight our flaws, making us feel like a dissected specimen under a microscope.

Yet, in a sense, they're right.

We still sin. We still make mistakes. We aren't perfect, but this doesn't extinguish God's love for us. He never lets go of His children. Nothing can steal us from Him, including our mistakes. We are forgiven sinners who experienced a heart transformation, not a heart perfectionism. We strive to be like Christ every day out of love for what He has done. Salvation and God's love aren't dependent upon our performance. Salvation can't be earned. It is God's free gift. How reassuring this is!

Action Discover peace in knowing that our perfection didn't save us. It can't. God doesn't love our perfectionism. He loves us. Your salvation is secured in Him. Don't stress about not being perfect. Strive to be like Christ every day, knowing you are loved beyond measure.

Catherine Cooley

Day Twenty-One

There are different kinds of gifts, but the same Spirit distributes them. There are different kinds of service, but the same Lord. There are different kinds of working, but in all of them and in everyone it is the same God at work. 1 Corinthians 12:4-6 (NIV)

"He is such a good preacher!" "When she praises God, it's like listening to an angel!"

Do you feel jealous when other Christians are praised? Does it make you feel insignificant, like you can't serve God how they do?

1 Corinthians 12 tells us that as Christians, we are each like one part of the body; without an ear, an eye, or a leg, the body suffers and isn't working at its best. Those who pour coffee, clean the floors, and arrange the church flowers all have a part to play, even if they work behind the scenes.

Because they get these tasks done, those who are in frontline work, such as the pastor, elders, and musicians, can focus on their callings by giving all their energy to where they serve. Being an active follower of Christ doesn't mean counting up your good deeds, and nobody has a more godly role than someone else. The body wouldn't be complete without each one of us serving in our place.

Action What gifts has God given you? How can you use them to glorify Him? Find a way to serve within your church and community, if you haven't already. Remember that God sees your heart and knows you are serving Him, even if nobody else notices.

Jessica Edwards

Day Twenty-Two

Every good and perfect gift is from above, coming down from the Father of the heavenly lights, who does not change like shifting shadows. He chose to give us birth through the word of truth, that we might be a kind of firstfruits of all he created.
James 1:17-18 (NIV)

When I was a toddler, my favorite animal in the world was a cat. And everyone knew it, especially my preschool teacher, Miss Lisa. One of my favorite things to do during free play was hunt down and play with a certain stuffed kitten. I can still remember the joy that filled my heart the day Miss Lisa let me take that kitten home to "babysit it"—and when she later told me I could look after it for good.

Just like Miss Lisa knew nothing would make me happier than that scruffy stuffed kitten, God knows the hopes and dreams in our own hearts. Likewise, He wants to give us good gifts that reflect both these desires and His will. But if our desires are different than His, then what will happen? How can we make our own earthly wants line up with His divine goals for us?

We can ask God to change our hearts! The more time we spend in deep communion with Him, the more our desires will align with His—and the more we'll see Him at work in our life.

Action Spend some time today in prayer, asking God how you can align your hopes and dreams with His will. Then, sit back and think about how you can use your own unique loves and passions to serve and honor Him.

Taylor Bennett

Day Twenty-Three

But from there you will seek the LORD your God and you will find him, if you search after him with all your heart and with all your soul.
Deuteronomy 4:29 (ESV)

I like to get in the ocean every day.

My mornings usually involve nursing my cuddly baby and kisses from Tobias and Adam. Once up, I step over laundry piles, ninja-navigate around toys, and head to the kitchen where I throw something in the blender as my hubby Adam makes coffee. Next, we either load into the truck (all four of us!) and head to the beach to check the surf and let the kids play while Adam and I take turns surfing, or I strike mission by myself for a couple of hours. If there are fun waves, I'm out there! If it's junky, I'll run the beach and do a workout on the sand. Either way, every day I'm training, getting ready for big waves that are coming. And not just ready; I want to dominate those waves, big or small. I want to feel the incredible thrill of being the best I can be on every wave.

Just like in surfing, I practice my faith daily, so when the moments of trial come, I am ready for the battle. If the big waves come and my muscles are flabby, it's too late, I'm going to get smoked or pounded. Or if the big trials of life come and I haven't been building my spiritual muscles, I am likely to get emotionally and spiritually wrecked.

So let's cling tight to Jesus every day because He is our ultimate muscle strengthener. He is the master of the daily, the author and finisher of our faith, and He has us in the palm of His hand. In Him, we are ready for the tough stuff in life. When you're unstoppable, each day is an opportunity to move closer to your dreams.

Action My unstoppable charge for today: master the daily and you will master your life. What simple life hacks, habits or mindsets help you keep going? What insights or ah-has did you glean from this, starting with the things you can put into action now?

Bethany Hamilton

Day Twenty-Four

"For my thoughts are not your thoughts, neither are your ways my ways," declares the LORD. "As the heavens are higher than the earth, so are my ways higher than your ways and my thoughts than your thoughts." Isaiah 55:8-9 (NIV)

'My thoughts are not your thoughts' – we don't think like God does. We are biased, opinionated, and judgmental. The Lord loves unconditionally.

'neither are your ways my ways' – we might not always like or understand what God does, but the chances are that if we were in His position it is exactly what we would choose to happen. Our perspective is like a zoomed-in camera, we just see our own life, situation, and circumstances. God's camera lens is not zoomed in – He can see the bigger picture, the whole landscape. The Lord can also see right from the beginning to the very end of our personal story. No detail is neglected or overlooked. Everything God does is for a purpose.

Jesus said, "I tell you the truth, unless a kernel of wheat falls to the ground and dies, it remains only a single seed. But if it dies, it produces many seeds." (John 12:24 NIV) What we go through might be painful, but God has a reason behind it, nothing happens by mistake.

Action Next time you get angry or upset and don't understand why something has happened the way it has, pray and ask God that one day, He will show you and you will be able to understand why.

Sophie Spree

Day Twenty-Five

This is what the LORD says: "Cursed is the one who trusts in man, who draws strength from mere flesh and whose heart turns away from the LORD. Jeremiah 17:5 (NIV)

Have you ever had a high expectation of someone? I mean you really looked up to this person as the shining example everyone ought to be? You confided in the person only to realize that it was all a lie? We often give people a role in our lives they never signed up for and so much power over us that whatever they say or do really affects us mostly negatively.

The problem is, we really want certain people to fit into this mold of a picture-perfect person with minimal faults, who always have our backs. These expectations are unrealistic because they often end in betrayal and with betrayal, comes the quest for revenge. Phew!

The reality is no one can fit into that picture-perfect category. Only GOD can. It is in Him we have our identity and only when we know Him and study his word then we become more like Him in words and deeds. We can totally trust and entrust our ups and downs to Him. We cannot control other people's behaviors, we can only control our own behaviors towards them.

It is time to release those who have offended you so that you can have peace. Sometimes, the offender might not be the problem but the one who is offended. How many people will you continue to avoid because of your search of the picture-perfect human that doesn't exist? Please take off all the undue expectations you've had of others and placed them on God. Let him heal your heart and give you a fresh start today. No matter what had happened in the past, it all happened so that you can learn from them.

Action Get a piece of paper and write out all the names of the people you need to forgive. Pray over this list each day until the poison leaves your system. Ask the Holy Spirit to help you let go of the past so that you can lay hold of God has in store for you.

Hannah Udobia

Day Twenty-Six

I sought the Lord and He heard me, and delivered me from all my fears.
Psalm 34:4 (NKJV)

There was about a year in my life where I struggled with intense anxiety. It was truly the hardest season I have ever experienced, and if you are struggling with anxiety too, my heart goes out to you. Anxiety and fear are a ploy of the devil that he uses to try to take ahold of our lives and his grip is very tight. But it's never too tight that Jesus cannot break it down.

Jesus made a way for me, He brought me out of the darkest place I have ever been, He fought the devil and now I am free to live for Him – and He can do the same for you.

Yes, I still struggle with anxiety sometimes. Everyone does, but it no longer controls me. And it doesn't have to control you either – you can claim victory over fear through Christ and His Word and have His beautiful peace that transcends all understanding.

Action Are you struggling with anxiety and fear? Reach out to someone today and have them pray with you and read through Scripture on the topic of overcoming through Christ. Write down your thoughts, prayers, and Scripture that encourages you most in a journal to keep for further use.

*It is very important to reach out if struggling mentally. If you need help, please reach out to someone you trust today. You are so important and loved.

Olivia Bell

Day Twenty-Seven

But now thus says the Lord, he who created you, O Jacob, he who formed you, O Israel: "Fear not, for I have redeemed you; I have called you by name, you are mine." Isaiah 43:1 (ESV)

One of the most exciting (and stressful) tasks of my life has been naming my children. Coming up with a name for a pet is one thing, but to name a human is quite another. That's the name they will have for their whole life... you don't want to mess that up! It really did feel like such a weighty responsibility, but it was also a great honor. Names carry meaning, distinguish us from others, and are how we are known in the world. After all, when meeting someone for the first time, the first piece of information we share is our name.

In the above verse, God says to Israel- His people- that He has redeemed them, called them by name, and that they are His. That is deeply personal and filled to the brim with loving-kindness. And just as God knew Israel by name, so He knows ours. Look at the beginning of that verse- what does it say? He formed and created us. He is our Maker who knows all of who we are. We are so loved. Even on the hardest days, we can rest in that truth, knowing God Almighty calls us by name.

Action Try to memorize the above verse! Write it on an index card and put it where you can see it. This is such a beautiful and powerful verse. If you ever need reminding of Who you belong to, read this verse and thank God for His magnificent love!

Nicole Byrum

Day Twenty-Eight

For by grace you have been saved through faith, and that not of yourselves: it is the gift of God, not of works, lest anyone should boast.
Ephesians 2:8-9 (NKJV)

We all love to receive gifts! Whether it be for birthdays, anniversaries, graduations, or even Christmas, we love gifts. The excitement and anticipation of unwrapping the paper and discovering what is inside is festive, and is usually surrounded by a celebration. Oftentimes, the love and friendship that is represented by the gift is even more precious to us.

God gave us the greatest gift: salvation. Being restored to a right relationship with God through the work of the cross allows us to have our sins forgiven and to have eternity with God. The Giver of the gift of the cross is Jesus! His blood that was shed, His death and resurrection, allows us to receive the greatest gift ever given…and allows us to recognize and thank the One who gave it.

Action Consider giving a small gift to someone you love. Ask the Lord to show you how to bless them and show your appreciation for them. Then pray and ask the Lord to help you recognize how many gifts He has given you!

Lori Findlaytor

Day Twenty-Nine

Lift your hands and give thanks to God for his marvelous kindness. Psalm 107:21 (TPT)

There was a time that I didn't feel like singing. We just got some news about our jobs, and the sudden economic downturn meant so many of our plans would be put on hold. A trip to England, which I had anticipated for months, suddenly canceled. The future looked unknown. I went on a walk to reflect on this, and as the sun warmed my face, God reminded me to keep singing. No matter the season, there is always a reason to praise Him. Even though it felt opposite to my feelings at the time, lifting up a song in this crisis drew me away from my problems to just focus on His presence.

Why worship when you don't feel like it?

Worship has a powerful effect: Paul and Silas were the only ones singing praise to God while in prison one night. I can't help but notice that they worshiped before their breakthrough, not just after! (Acts 16:22-31)

Worship involves our whole being: Engage your body, mind, and heart in praise. It helps to release emotions stored up. Lifting hands is an act of surrender. It communicates that we believe He is Lord.

My energetic two-year-old reminds me it's always a good time to praise. Since learning the Doxology (which we sing at our church), she will break out in song.. even at dinner!

Action Don't wait until your circumstances change to worship God. Bring Him praise in the midst of whatever you're facing. Start with this beautiful hymn:

Praise God from whom all blessings flow
Praise him, all creatures here below
Praise him above, ye heavenly host
Praise Father, Son, and Holy Ghost
Amen.

Becca Nicholson

Day Thirty

The point is this: whoever sows sparingly will also reap sparingly, and whoever sows bountifully will also reap bountifully. 2 Corinthians 9:6 (ESV)

Seeds can grow into new plants. No one multiplies without sowing seeds. Even you are a product of seed sown years ago. When you preserve a seed, you have preserved a generation.

A harvest is a reflection of the seeds that started it beforehand. You can only reap what you sow. When we sow the Gospel seed into a prepared heart, it will begin to germinate and grow with the heart, because the seed carries life. Our duty as Christians is to preach the word (sow the seed) into the hearts of others. Then it can germinate.

The farmer can only plant the seed and water it. He has no control over how it germinates. It may take days, months, or even years for a seed to germinate, but when planted in the right condition, something is bound to happen. Your evangelism is not a waste, keep sowing!

The decisions we make, time spent, and actions we take are seeds. Make the right decisions, invest your time wisely, and take the corresponding action, and you will have a fruitful future for a harvest.

Action Realize that every action you take is a seed growing for harvest in the future. What actions are you making today that could result in a future bountiful harvest?

Emmanuel Olapade

Day Thirty-One

Come to Me, all who are weary and heavy-laden, and I will give you rest. Take My yoke upon you and learn from Me, for I am gentle and humble in heart, and you will find rest for your souls. Matthew 11:28-29 (NASB)

In the Old Testament, God's people were given a list of rules on how to come to the Tabernacle of the Lord. In Exodus, we read about all the different offerings required to pay for sin and the purifying rituals to make the Jews right with God.

Take a look at the contrast in the verse from Matthew above as Jesus says to the crowd, 'Come to me…' He is inviting us to simply come. Because of Jesus' life on earth and His death and resurrection, we no longer have to sacrifice animals to purify ourselves. We have Jesus' love, forgiveness and a relationship with Him at our fingertips. No more barrier between God and man. When Jesus was born a human, He broke down that wall!

Now we are simply invited to come. Every shortcoming and fear can be left at the feet of Jesus. He will refresh us just as He promised, 'you will find rest for your souls'.

Action We have nothing stopping us coming to the God of the universe, so why do we hesitate? Actively make time to rest in God's presence today, somewhere away from distractions. Listen to a hymn, pray aloud a Psalm, or simply sit and marvel at the God who made everything – yet sees you and cares about every worry on your heart. Breathe in His peace.

Jessica Edwards

Day Thirty-Two

For ever since the world was created, people have seen the earth and sky. Through everything God made, they can clearly see his invisible qualities – his eternal power and divine nature. So they have no excuse for not knowing God. Romans 1:20 (NLT)

I was struck one morning by how pretty things like frost, ice, and snow are, and yet how dangerous they can also be. Then my mind went to campfires. I find staring into campfires mesmerizing. Campfires are pretty but can be dangerous. Large bodies of water are pretty, however, water could be dangerous if it's deeper than you expect, or if it gets stormy.

It's ok to find all these natural things like fire and water pretty, as long as we have a healthy respect for them at the same time.

This is much like God.

We sing worship songs to Him like 'You're Beautiful', but we still need to have a healthy amount of fear, respect, and awe for Him.

There's a quote in C.S. Lewis' book *The Lion, The Witch And The Wardrobe* where Mr. Beaver says (about Aslan, the lion): "'course he isn't safe. But he's good."

This is like God. He may not always seem safe, but He is always good and He is always just.

Action How do you view God? Do you see Him as just a friend or someone who can give you what you want when you pray? Or do you remember that He is holy and have respect for Him at the same time as remembering He is your friend? Pray about seeing God for all He is.

Sophie Spree

Day Thirty-Three

So the sisters sent to Him, saying, "Lord, he whom you love is ill…" Now Jesus loved Martha and her sister and Lazarus. So, when He heard Lazarus was ill, He stayed two days longer in the place where He was.
John 11:3, 5-6 (ESV)

Have you ever felt like God isn't paying attention to you? You are in great need of holy intervention. You have called out to the Lord daily in prayer, but still haven't gotten any answer? I can imagine that is exactly how Mary and Martha felt, or even more so, Lazarus.

We see how clearly, Jesus *loved* them. When he heard that they needed him, why would he wait? In our minds, the most natural thing is to rush to the aid of those in need, like Superman when he hears the cry of a civilian in trouble. That, however, is not how Jesus responded. In fact, by the time Jesus did arrive, all hope had been lost.

It was finished… the time for rescue had come and gone. The worst had happened, and there was no need anymore. The person that needed saving was already lost. Why would Jesus do this? Did he not know their need? Did he not care about them? Did the death of Lazarus take him by surprise? At this point, Lazarus had been dead four long days!

This loving Jesus, the miracle worker, the Messiah! <u>Four. Days. Late.</u>

Jesus told them to roll away the stone, and called into the tomb. Lazarus awoke! He was… ALIVE! And many who saw what happened believed.

Action Maybe you feel like Jesus is late. All hope is *gone*. You prayed, you had faith, but he didn't show. Or maybe when he did show, all you could think was "It's too late! Why wait so long?". Remember he has a plan and works all things for his glory. He is the author, and we are characters in His story. He can use this heartbreak to show His power so that others would come to faith in Him. You may feel lost and don't understand how things could be good after so much wrong has happened, but remember: Even when He's four days late, He's still on time!

Nathan Johnson

Day Thirty-Four

She is clothed with strength and dignity, and she laughs without fear of the future. When she speaks, her words are wise, and she gives instructions with kindness. Proverbs 31:25-26 (NLT)

Characteristics make us who we are. Your friend may be athletic, your grandma may be patient, your father may be wise, you might be artistic. Everybody has a different personality. Most aspects of our personalities are great. But oftentimes, we get lost in the busyness of the world, and we struggle to hold on to who we are. We'd rather be popular or liked, rather than kind and compassionate.

Lots of teens, even adults, look at what others have and long to be like that. And as soon as they achieve it, they move on to the next thing they want. But you have those qualities because that is how God made you. He didn't design you with a compassionate heart and a wise mind just so you could wish that you were gorgeous and popular. Every characteristic you possess serves a purpose. They are tools in a toolbox. Each tool serves a different purpose, and, in time, you will need and use every single one.

You'll probably always want to switch out this tool or that tool for someone else's. You may even wish to get a whole new toolbox. But someone else's tools aren't going to fit you. Your tools were custom made specifically for you by the Master Creator, Artist, and Author. And He sees into your future, so He should know which tools will come in handy. It's like getting a craft kit. As you're unpacking it, you find a piece in the box and think, "What in the world could that be for? There's no way I'll need it." Then you get to the middle of the project and realize the whole thing would literally fall apart if you didn't have that one tool. The maker knew you would need it. God knows what you need too. Trust Him, and He will guide you.

Action Put up Proverbs 31:25-26 in your room. If you're a guy, feel free to change 'she' to 'he'. Recite it to yourself each morning and night. This will remind you of the important qualities of a person. Each time you find yourself longing for something someone else has, recite the verse and ask God to help you be content with who you are and what you have.

Kaitlyn Giesbrecht

Day Thirty-Five

By faith in the name of Jesus, this man whom you see and know was made strong. It is Jesus' name and the faith that comes through him that has completely healed him, as you can all see. **Acts 3:16 (NIV)**

Do you believe in miracles? I sure do. I have heard and experienced the healing power of God.

At the age of three, my little brother almost died. He was extremely sick just came back from the hospital. All of a sudden, he couldn't breathe and was burning in fever. We all thought he was going to die. My grandfather took him and began to pray over him. Suddenly, he started to breathe and his fever started to drop. By the time the ambulance came, he was awake and talking. If that is not a miracle, I don't know what is.

Another miracle that always amazes me is when a ton of steel fell on my grandfather when he was only 23. He was in the hospital for six months and they didn't think he was going to make it. Well, he did! Imagine his story featured in a newspaper. Years later, he was told that he would die in six months from leukemia. Well, he didn't. He successfully underwent a bone marrow transplant and was cancer-free to the day God called him to His Kingdom. He sadly passed away at the age 72, but lived a long, blessed life and never complained. My grandfather's life always inspires me. He was a man of faith who believed and testified about the goodness of God. His faith resulted in miracle after miracle.

As for me, I've had my own health challenges early on in my life. I can testify that it has been more than 2 years since I have had to step into an ER. That is huge.

No matter what seems impossible, we have to believe and have faith in God that He is a God of miracles.

Action **Pray and have faith that God is in control. When you need a miracle, cast out all your fears and doubts, trusting that nothing is impossible for God.**

Tiara Cirino

Day Thirty-Six

I have hidden your word in my heart that I might not sin against you.
Psalm 119:11 (NIV)

"Why do you have to be so..." I stopped shouting mid-sentence.

Encourage one another and build each other up (1 Thessalonians 5:11a, NIV). The verse popped into my mind before I could stop it. Yelling at my brother certainly wasn't encouraging and up-building. I took a deep breath and started the sentence again in a calm and thought-through way.

The psalmist in the verse above says that he memorizes God's word so that it can stop him from sinning. That is exactly what I experienced. A verse I had "hidden in my heart" as a child came back to me in the right moment and it stopped me from sinning.

Action Memorize a verse of the Bible today. 1 Thessalonians 5:11 is a good one to start, "Therefore encourage one another and build each other up, just as in fact you are doing." (NIV)

Sarah Susanna Rhomberg

Day Thirty-Seven

May the favor of the Lord our God rest on us; establish the work of our hands for us- yes, establish the work of our hands. Psalm 90:17 (NIV)

How many times have you been asked, "What do you want to do when you grow up?" That can be a difficult question to answer! When I was in high school, I was interested in pharmacy. However, I changed my mind about that, and when I went to college I was undecided in my major. I considered majoring in theology, missions, or even English before I settled on psychology. Even as an adult, there have been times I questioned what I should be doing vocation-wise. Until recently, writing had not even been a part of my career!

There is value in evaluating our interests and talents when considering what to do with our lives. However, it's not up to us to "get it just right." The Bible tells us that God has good works for us to do which he has already prepared (Ephesians 2:10). Furthermore, the Bible also tells us that no plans of the Lord can be thwarted (Job 42:2). This means that God will providentially direct our paths and that nothing can ruin what he has purposed! When we trust God, we can be assured that He will establish the work of our hands.

Action When you find yourself feeling anxious about the future, turn to the 3 verses mentioned here: Psalm 90:17, Ephesians 2:10, and Job 42:2. Take time to praise God that He has called you to good works. Ask Him to help you trust in His established plans.

Nicole Byrum

Day Thirty-Eight

Watch, stand fast in the faith, be brave, be strong. Let all that you do be done with love. 1 Corinthians 16:13-14 (NKJV)

Difficult days are a part of life. Everyone has them. No is immune to trials. What we choose to do in those trials, how we act and react, is what makes or breaks us.

Jesus was not exempt from challenges. People often ridiculed Him, accused Him, and even rejected and abandoned Him. Yet when we look at His life, we see that everything He did, He did with love for His Father in Heaven, and His love for us.

You may feel all alone in your struggles, but you are not alone. Jesus sees you and loves you. He gives you the strength to be brave and strong. Your response to Him is to do all things in love. Love for Him, love for your family and friends, and even love for yourself! The little things become significant things when done in love.

Action Take a moment to reflect on the tasks that you do every day. How can you show the love of Jesus in those tasks? Now, think of a task that seems too difficult or too large. How can you be strong in this task? How can God help you to be brave? Let His love lead you and guide you.

Lori Findlaytor

Day Thirty-Nine

Be kind and compassionate to one another, forgiving each other, just as in Christ God forgave you. Ephesians 4:32 (NLT)

I was babysitting a foster family's new toddler. After getting him settled in his bed for naptime, I also relaxed. I chose a comfy chair in their living room, right next to an end table that featured framed photos of every child the couple had ever fostered. One of the pictures caught my eye.

The photo was old, but it was clearly a picture of one of my gym classmates. But this wasn't just any classmate. He was clumsy and socially awkward, which was not a good combination for the team games we played in physical education. Several classmates teased him and called him names. Although I wasn't leading the name-calling, I often joined in the laughter to blend in. I certainly never tried sticking up for him.

I didn't know this guy's full story, and I never pried to find out. But I do know that moving in and out of foster homes can be stressful and life-changing, even years later. Being in high school is tough enough without the past he had, but the jeering in the gym likely only made his struggles worse.

That day, I was convicted. Jesus and his disciples often spoke against using harsh words and name-calling. Although most of them in turn were mocked or even cruelly killed, they never retaliated. I needed to follow their example.

The next week in gym, instead of laughing like everyone else, I frowned at the remarks made. When this classmate tried talking to me, we engaged in real conversation. Eventually, the teasing tapered off. When our team played class sports, we could finally all support each other instead of tearing each other down.

Action Is there anyone in your life who you are not treating the same way Jesus would? Make a difference in your attitude and actions today.

Jessica Lippe

Day Forty

Create in me a clean heart, O God, and renew a steadfast spirit within me.
Psalm 51:10 (NIV)

A study once showed that around 80% of people fail to keep the New Year resolutions that they make.

At the time of writing this, New Year seems a very long time ago, and in all honesty, I barely remember what, if any, New Year's resolutions I told myself I would make. And you know what? That's okay! A lot of people put a lot of pressure on themselves to suddenly make their lives perfect from 1st January onwards. Changes like that don't happen overnight.

The verse above says, 'Create in me a clean heart, O God, and renew a steadfast spirit within me.' Pray like David, the psalmist that wrote that. When we allow God to clean our hearts, we will focus less on keeping resolutions and seek God's will and His guidance more in everything we do.

Another great verse to pray, that David also wrote, is 'May the words of my mouth and the meditation of my heart [that's your thoughts] be pleasing to you, O LORD, my rock and my redeemer.' (Psalm 19:14 NLT)

Action Listen to the song 'Create In Me' by Rend Collective. Reflect on the words and spend some time thanking God that He is not finished with you yet.

Sophie Spree

Day Forty-One

I praise you for I am fearfully and wonderfully made. Wonderful are your works; my soul knows it very well. Psalm 139:14 (ESV)

The creator of the universe, the one and only God, made you to be a wonderful person. Think about that for a second.

Lots of us struggle with self-image. We drag ourselves down or inflate our accomplishments. But God doesn't want us to do either. He wants us to take an honest assessment of our hearts, lives, and actions. It's not always easy. Sometimes we would rather believe we are better than we really are, or we choose to believe the negative comments we've received. God wants us to improve ourselves for His glory. He wants us to strive every day to be a little bit better than we were yesterday. And there's no way we can do that on our own. We have to ask for God's help. All He's waiting for is that little whisper, "I need Your help", that little prayer in the back of our minds admitting that we can't do it by ourselves. He wants to help. He needs that invitation. God will never take away your free will, and that's why it's so important to ask for His help in being honest with ourselves.

So today, right now, I encourage you to step back, take a breath, and take an honest and realistic assessment of yourself. Is your heart where it should be? Are you trying your hardest to do the right thing? Are you trying to do the right thing just because you *should,* or because that's what God wants you to do? These questions are hard, but they're crucial to mature in your faith and become the person God made you to be. *You* are fearfully and wonderfully made, so strive, today and every day, to be who you were created to be.

Action Pray, "God, I know you made me wonderfully and fearfully. Thank you for that. God, give me the strength to be honest with myself and where I need to improve. Help me to become who you created to me. Lord, you know my heart, and you know where I need help, so help me. Thank you for all of your blessings. I love you. Amen."

Kaitlyn Giesbrecht

Day Forty-Two

This is the [remarkable degree of] confidence which we [as believers are entitled to] have before Him: that if we ask anything according to His will, [that is, consistent with His plan and purpose] He hears us. 1 John 5:14 (AMP)

Oftentimes when we pray, we're not really expecting God to answer. We have a lack of faith; we ask with a heart as unstable as water. Prayer of faith is not asking for a thing, it is believing that you are a possessor of that thing.

Jesus is our perfect example. He prayed a prayer of faith "I knew that you always hear me and listen to me." (John 11:42, AMP) He believed the Father will hear Him even before asking. That's how we should pray. He wasn't struggling to be heard by the Father nor waiting for answers, He knew the answer was with Him.

God is ready to graciously give us all things (see Romans 8:32). A faith-sponsored prayer is praying with the consciousness of the finished work of Christ.

Action Stop asking with fear or timidity. God is your Father. Walk up to Him and ask with boldness, He is a loving Father.

Emmanuel Olapade

Day Forty-Three

*For the L*ORD *sees not as man sees: man looks on the outward appearance, but the L*ORD *looks on the heart.* 1 Samuel 16:7b (ESV)

If you're anything like me, you want people to like you. I have spent so much energy hoping people would like me more.

Often comparing myself to others who seem more cool, pretty, or popular. When I was 17, I was a junior counselor at a summer camp. The girls in my dorm were so cool. I wanted so badly to fit in with them. The purpose of the camp was to set aside several weeks to spend time with God. There were some rules to follow for our safety and to minimize distractions.

Soon after camp started, our counselor started to encourage the students to break rules. After that, the main focus for our dorm was breaking as many rules as possible without getting caught. It was a game. I went to our counselor and told her I didn't agree with what was going on. I was so torn when she didn't listen to me.

"What should I do?" I thought. I didn't want to tattle on everyone. I asked God what he wanted me to do. I wanted people to like me, but I realized I needed to do what was right; even if it meant people wouldn't like me. So I told the dean and she put a stop to it.

When we focus on people's opinions of us, we lose sight of what God says. We start listening to what others think and stop listening to what God wants for us. Instead, let's ask God what he wants each day of our life to look like. When you are faced with hard or awkward situations you can ask God for guidance.

Action Let's pray together: Dear Lord, please teach me how to live my life focused on you. Will you show me what you want me to do today and help me to see myself the way you see me? Thank you for your love and direction. Amen.

Hahnna Tokich

Day Forty-Four

A new commandment I give to you, that you love one another: just as I have loved you, you also are to love one another. John 13:34 (ESV)

We are living in a time when we are seeing things that we never imagined we would see in our lifetime. There are people who take actions based on the way we look, where we come from, or what we have. However, the reality is that we were all created in God's perfect image and that God loves us just the way we are. We all fall short of the glory of God.

Unfortunately, there are times that people don't see that we are all equal and we all bleed the same blood. Some people only see color. That is what we call racism. The Bible talks about how God created us in His own image. We were created in God's perfect image. No matter how we look or what we have, we are loved by God. We were called for such a time as this. God loves you whether you're black, white, Latino, Asian, or any other race. All He cares about is that we love Him, serve Him, and treat others with love.

As Christians, we must love one another and show the love of Christ to everyone. As a Puerto Rican-American girl, I have had to deal with so many challenges with racism by peers and even harder my fellow Christian friends. At age 10, I've heard people say, "she's Hispanic, she is probably poor and has no money." It hurts that I have had to deal with this. Unfortunately, blacks in America have been dealing with many challenges with racism for hundreds of years. Now more than ever, as Christians we need to lead by example. We must treat people with the love and respect. We must show God's love to everyone, especially in times of crisis. We must also know that if we ever deal with any type of racism or mistreatment, that we are uniquely and wonderfully made in God's perfect image. That should not shake us.

Action Make sure to follow the ten commandments. Read the Bible and learn more about what God has to say about treating people with love. If you have ever been racist or made judgments based on your own assumptions, pray and ask for forgiveness. One of the best ways to show God's love is to love one another like Christ loved the church.

Tiara Cirino

Day Forty-Five

But Ruth replied, "Don't urge me to leave you or to turn back from you. Where you go I will go, and where you stay I will stay. Your people will be my people and your God my God. Ruth 1:16 (NIV)

Ruth understood something that is incredibly important. She was on the way back to Israel with her mother-in-law when she made the well-known statement. One phrase in it is key: Your God is my God.

Ruth, who had grown up with heathen idols, understood that the God of Israel was the only true God. But there is more. She understood that God must become her God.

I was born into a Christian family. I never struggled with doubting that the God of the Bible is the true God. But that didn't make me a Christian. It was only when I declared that God is not only the *true* God, but *my God*, that my relationship with Him started.

Action Is God *your* God? Have you declared Him as that? Make Ruth's statement your prayer: "God, you are my God."

Sarah Susanna Rhomberg

Day Forty-Six

All these are the work of one and the same Spirit; and he gives them to each one, just as he determines. 1 Corinthians 12:11 (NIV)

Have you ever noticed other people's talents and abilities have a way of seeming better than your own? I don't know about you, but for me, it's easy to fall into the trap of comparing myself to others. Somehow, I never seem to measure up. The truth is, all of those comparisons leave me feeling weak, insecure, and inadequate. Thankfully, the Apostle Paul gave us some wise words to consider whenever we're faced with the temptation to compare.

In 1 Corinthians chapter 12, Paul writes about the spiritual gifts given to God's children. Make no mistake, these gifts are very different from one another! But they all have one thing in common- they are all the work of the Holy Spirit for the benefit of the church. Paul then uses an analogy of the human body, emphasizing the need for every part. Likewise, the body of Christ- the church- is made up of many parts, each one of vital importance.

This means God has uniquely gifted us for a role to play in His kingdom! Rather than compare ourselves to others, we can rest in the truth that God has designated our gifts and abilities just as He determined.

Action When you find that you are comparing yourself to others, stop and reread 1 Corinthians chapter 12. Thank God for the way He has gifted you, and for the work He has called you to do!

Nicole Byrum

Day Forty-Seven

Why am I discouraged? Why is my heart so sad? I will put my hope in God! I will praise Him again- my Savior and my God! Psalm 42:11 NLT

Some days it feels like our emotions control us, rather than us controlling our emotions. Some days it is just plain hard not to be discouraged. We go through difficult times, challenges with school and work, struggles with family and friends. It is easy to lose sight of what is really important, our relationship with God!

King David went through challenges as well. He felt scared and alone, and very discouraged! He was frustrated and cried out to God. He admitted he was sad and had no problem telling God exactly how he felt! But David didn't stay in that emotional place of discouragement and sadness. He found the remedy and began to put his hope in God, to praise Him, and to speak the truth of who God was over the emotions of his heart. He declared the reality of who God was to him, "my Savior and my God."

Action When we begin to speak out the truth of who God is, our emotions come into agreement with that truth. Maybe not right away, but eventually. Today, begin to remind yourself of who God is to you… friend, Savior, redeemer, wonderful counselor, Prince of peace!

Lori Findlaytor

Day Forty-Eight

Come now, you who say, "Today or tomorrow we will travel to such and such a city and spend a year there and do business and make a profit." You don't even know what tomorrow will bring- what your life will be!
James 4:13-14a (HCSB)

I spent five months planning for an 11-week trip overseas. Every conversation I had turned to me telling people about the 11 different countries I was going to visit and all the iconic sites I was going to see, like the Swiss Alps, the Last Supper, the Berlin Wall, and Anne Frank's House. When the day of my departure finally arrived, I felt a bit unsettled. But I figured it was just nerves of excitement as I boarded the plane.

Covid-19 had just begun its global spread. I soon had to cancel the few days I was planning in Italy, but at the time it didn't look like the rest of my trip would be affected. However, it wasn't long before tourist attractions closed, travel was discouraged, and I had a close call leaving a country just before the accommodations and borders of that country closed down! I knew then that I wouldn't be able to stay for all 11 weeks. I got a ticket to go home after I'd only seen two countries in three weeks. The rest of my vacation time was spent quarantined at home.

Through all this, I spent a lot of time asking God why. Why would he let a virus spread that would take so many lives and affect so many others? More selfishly, I asked why I had to work so hard and so long to plan and pay for that trip, only to have my plans torn to pieces.

I'd heard several scripture passages explaining how God is the only one who can make plans that won't fail, but I had never seen it play out in my life so accurately. The entire time, I had been trying to justify my own travel plans, but they weren't God's plan. I still don't have all the answers why this tragedy occurred, but in my own life, I learned to let the Lord be the master plan maker, not a consultant for approval.

Action It's okay to ask God why. Take a moment right now to ask about anything on your mind. Just make sure to keep your eyes and ears open for when God answers your question.

Jessica Lippe

Day Forty-Nine

Let the heavens rejoice, let the earth be glad; let the sea resound, and all that is in it. Psalm 96:11 (NIV)

In this day and age, it could be hard to 'rejoice' and 'be glad' when we see all the terrible things happening in the world. (As an example, I am writing this during lockdown because of the COVID-19 pandemic.) But the previous verse in the Psalm says, 'Say among the nations "The LORD reigns." The world is firmly established, it cannot be moved; he will judge the peoples with equity.' (Psalm 96:10 NIV).

'The world is firmly established, it cannot be moved;' this is why we can 'rejoice' and 'be glad' because we know we are safe and secure in the Lord's hands.

In Psalm 56 David writes, 'in God I trust and am not afraid. What can man do to me?' (Psalm 56:11 NIV) This is a great Bible verse to remember.

Action Write one of these verses down now – on a post-it-note, on your phone, anywhere! Next time you feel afraid about something, reread the verse and claim the truth of it for yourself.

Sophie Spree

Day Fifty

For am I now seeking the approval of man, or of God? Or am I trying to please man? If I were still trying to please man, I would not be a servant of Christ. Galatians 1:10 (ESV)

"You can be friends with her, or you can be friends with us!"

As the new kid in school, making friends was hard and I was now being faced with an ultimatum. When I moved, I was befriended by the 'popular' girls and would hang out with them often. However, I was also friends with a girl who wore long skirts and had uncut hair of her family's faith preferences. She was like everyone else. And no one really accepted her.

The 'popular' girls didn't want anyone in their group to be friends with her. So, they told me I could either stay friends with them *or* I could be her friend. I had to make a choice.

The easy choice would've been to stay in the 'popular' crowd, but that wouldn't have been the right one. I felt God pulling me in another direction and decided to obey Him.

That girl in the long skirts became one of my best friends!

But I would be lying if I told you that is all that happened. Those popular girls were not nice to me. They bullied me. I felt so left out sometimes. It was hard. But, looking back, that decision was one of the most important ones of my entire life, It has helped me become the woman I am today, one who seeks God's approval above everyone else.

Action I know it can seem scary and often lonely to break apart from the crowd to follow Christ, but God made you strong. He gave you the power to stand up for what you believe in and promises that you will never be alone because He is always with you. Know this: God does not break His promises.

Anonymous

Day Fifty-One

But rise, and stand upon thy feet: for I have appeared unto thee for this purpose, to make thee a minister and a witness both of these things which thou hast seen, and of those things in the which I will appear unto thee; delivering thee from the people, and from the Gentiles, unto whom now I send thee, To open their eyes, and to turn them from darkness to light, and from the power of Satan unto God, that they may receive forgiveness of sins, and inheritance among them which are sanctified by faith that is in me. Acts 26:16-18 (KJV)

The Gospel simply means good news. In this dying world, you need to proclaim the undying love of God to others.

Every believer has been called to the great commission: Go therefore and make disciples of all nations (Matthew 28:19). This is not a commission just for pastors, apostles, and those who wear a suit and tie to preach on our pulpit. Rather, it is a commitment to every believer.

Jesus commanded us to go and make. He didn't tell us to stay and sleep. Sharing the Gospel is a call to responsibility. We need to get ourselves ready, stand up, and say what the Lord commands.

Just like how no one can catch a fish sitting in his house, you need to go out and fish for men. Go and make disciples by evangelizing.

Action Think about one person you know who doesn't know the Lord. Look for ways to tell him or her about God's love this week.

Emmanuel Olapade

Day Fifty-Two

"Come, follow me," Jesus said, "and I will make you fishers of men."
Matthew 4:19 (BSB)

Learning the sport of fishing can symbolize Jesus' call to evangelize. There is a lot that goes into fishing. Fishing, like my family does, requires preparation up until the worm hits the water. We have to get the boat ready ahead of time and pack snacks, sandwiches, and sunscreen. We fill the boat with gas and find the good fishing spots on the lake. And even with all the prep, there is still the essential quality every fisherman must have: patience.

Evangelizing, or sharing the gospel, is a lot like that. There is prepping we must do ahead of time. To prepare our hearts to share about Jesus, we must know Him ourselves. How do we get to know Him better? By reading the Word, praying, and finding fellowship with friends that encourage the growth of our relationship with Jesus.

When we go out and share with others what Jesus has done in our lives, we still might not see an immediate response. This is where we place our patience and trust in Jesus.

This must be one reason why Jesus called ordinary fisherman to come follow Him. They understood hard work, preparation, and patience well.

Action Think of something Jesus might be calling you to drop in order to pick up His call to evangelize.

Britney Froese

Day Fifty-Three

Do everything without complaining or arguing, so that you may become blameless and pure, children of God without fault in a crooked and depraved generation, in which you shine like stars in the universe.
Philippians 2:14-15 (NIV)

When my husband and I first started dating, we were spending time with his family in Twelve Mile, Indiana. I'm guessing you've never heard of this town- after all, the population just reaches 200 people. In fact, the first time I visited his childhood home, I told him it smelled like the fair. He called me a "townie" in return (a joke that still continues to this day).

Around 10:00 pm, he asked me if I wanted to go for a walk with him around his parents' farm. I hesitated at first on account of the chilly weather, but after a while, he convinced me. I'm sure glad he did. Against the darkness of the country night sky, the stars were simply amazing. There were so many of them and they were so bright! Living in town all my life, I had never seen stars quite like this.

It's awesome to think we shine like those stars when we choose to do all things without complaining. It's the norm in everyday life to hear grumbling and arguing. As followers of Jesus, we are called to live with gratitude and joy! And when we do so, we shine brighter than the country stars.

Action If you're feeling crafty, cut out and color some stars to hang up in your room (or in your locker at school). Let them be a reminder to do everything without complaining or arguing. Or, when you're tempted to complain, simply close your eyes and envision the country stars!

Nicole Byrum

Day Fifty-Four

A man with leprosy came to him and begged him on his knees, "If you are willing, you can make me clean." Jesus was indignant. He reached out his hand and touched the man. "I am willing," he said. "Be clean!" Mark 1:40-41 (NIV)

Leprosy was a hideous disease. It not only made a person detestable to look at but, because of how contagious is it was, it also made him untouchable. Perhaps that was the worst part of it all—never being touched by those you love the most. The heartache must have unspeakable.

Jesus most often healed people by just saying a word. He called Lazarus out of the grave, gave thanks for the bread that fed the 5,000, and told the invalid to get up, pick up his mat and walk.

However, for the leper that came to Him on this day, Jesus doesn't merely command the disease to leave. He looks at this man, broken, desolate, and without hope. Then He does the unthinkable.

He reaches out His hand, and then He touches him. Only after this does He bid the leprosy to depart.

Jesus gave him much more than he had asked for. He healed him of leprosy, but in touching his body, Jesus touched his heart as well.

Action If you ever feel broken, desolate and without hope like the leper in this story, be assured that you will never be untouchable in God's eyes.

John Pasquet

Day Fifty-Five

I long to see you so that I may impart to you some spiritual gift to make you strong -- that is, that you and I may be mutually encouraged by each other's faith. Romans 1:11-12 (NIV)

I met my best friends in college. We did everything together; studied together, stayed up late laughing together, cried together, prayed together. After college, we all went our separate ways, and now we live in four different states! Thankfully, we still keep in touch, and we all talk about once a month. These times that we have set apart to 'be' together (whether physically or virtually) are so refreshing. By sharing our lives, we are able to encourage, uplift, and challenge one another. I often leave these conversations revitalized and encouraged that there are other believers cheering me on and walking the walk with me.

Paul felt the same towards the believers in Rome. He longed to be with them so that they could encourage each other.

The Christian life is not meant to be walked alone. God commands us to meet together with other believers because He knows that we need each other. He created us for human connection. The church is the body of Christ, and the body works best when all of the parts are working together. What a gift it is to be a part of that!

Action Do you have a community of believers around you? If so, reach out to them and thank them for their mutual encouragement in your life. If not, think about the people in your life who are believers, and reach out to them to start a relationship! There is no telling where a friendship might blossom if we choose to step out.

Annie Joransen

Day Fifty-Six

You, God, are my God, earnestly I seek you; I thirst for you, my whole being longs for you, in a dry and parched land where there is no water.
Psalm 63:1 (NIV)

'O God, you are my God,' is a statement of proclamation, acknowledging and declaring who God is.

'earnestly I seek you;' this comes as a challenge, do I earnestly seek God and put Him first, making an effort and keeping my priorities straight?

'my soul thirsts for you, my body longs for you, in a dry and parched land where there is no water.' This is a good metaphor, using very visual language. Imagine being in a barren, sparse desert land, stranded. You'd give anything for a long cold drink of water. Our desire for God should be as great as that.

Action Picture the empty desert scene again. Imagine that as life without God. It is in stark contrast to life with God. Jesus says, "I have come that they may have life, and have it to the full." John 10:10 NIV) that is completely opposite to the desert. What Jesus promises there is luscious and abundant. Choose life with God today.

Sophie Spree

Day Fifty-Seven

I have much to write to you, but I do not want to use paper and ink. Instead, I hope to visit you and talk with you face to face, so that our joy may be complete. 2 John 1:12 (NIV)

If our time during the COVID-19 quarantine taught us anything, it's how much we need our friends. Most of our communication is done through our phones these days. Texting, messaging, and social media: it's how we live.

But read this verse again. How is our joy made complete? How do we feel most happy and alive? Paul says it's through talking with our friends and loved ones face-to-face.

God knew texting alone couldn't satisfy us. In fact, too much texting and not enough face time actually brings us down. Paul knew writing letters wasn't enough to fill him up personally. He needed to see his friends so he could be encouraged. He wanted to talk, laugh, and pray with them, just like us. Paul wanted to be filled with joy, as do we, and that comes through face-to-face time with those we love.

Action Set up a night with your friends. Stay in and watch movies and play games or go to your favorite hangout spot. It doesn't matter. Just get together for a night of laughing, encouraging, and loving on each other in Christ.

Lea Vaverchak

Day Fifty-Eight

For everything there is a season, and a time for every matter under heaven. Ecclesiastes 3:1 (ESV)

Have you ever wondered just what God is doing in your life? Maybe you're in a time of uncertainty where you don't know what to do, you're waiting for answers that haven't come, or it seems as though God has forgotten all about you. Wherever you are in your life and your walk with God, know that there is a season for everything.

God is all-knowing and sees the big picture, while we can only see the tiniest part of his plan! It is amazing to look back on a time of struggle or uncertainty and see how God was working and moving, even if it seemed like he was silent at the time. God hasn't forgotten about you! Trust his timing and pray that he will guide you.

Action Rest in the truth of the Bible that God has a plan for you! He is all-knowing and all-powerful, and his timing is perfect.

Talia Ward

Day Fifty-Nine

For You formed my inward parts; You wove me in my mother's womb.
Psalm 139:13 (NASB)

At eighteen, I lost myself. I became someone I didn't recognize anymore, in a desperate attempt to fit in and feel wanted.

My life spiraled into a heap of confusion, wrong choices, and a broken heart. I learned a valuable lesson; my focus was so off-center that I looked to the world for my self-esteem and value.

In truth, I needed to look to God to know who I am. It's easy to get caught up in the social media hype or the trail of picture-perfect celebrities that we miss the need to refocus and remember the Creator who made us – just the way we are.

When I have doubts, I listen to 'My worth is not in what I own', by Keith and Kristyn Getty, and I remember that only God knows my true value.

Action Write out the Bible verse above and stick it somewhere you'll see it every day – a mirror, door, or as a screensaver on your phone. Set your focus on Jesus when the world threatens to overwhelm your sense of self-worth.

Jessica Edwards

Day Sixty

Be joyful in hope, patient in affliction, faithful in prayer. Romans 12:12 (NIV)

Ingredients in a recipe are critical for success. Chocolate cake is delicious because…well, because of the ingredients. Each item mixes together to form the finished product. If something is missing, you know it!

Life has ingredients too: family, friends, and, most important, God. In His faithfulness, God has given us a "recipe" for life. Romans 12:12 tells us to be joyful in hope. Joy is based on an internal decision rather than an external circumstance. Next is patient in affliction. We will have challenging times in life, but we have to add patience to the daily mix. Last is faithful in prayer. Talking to God, and doing it often, allows us to pour out our concerns, doubts, and fears to Him. We open up our hearts to receive mercy, grace, and wisdom from Him.

When we follow this "recipe" for life, God is able to move in us and through us for our benefit and for His glory!

Action Ask the Lord if any of the "ingredients" (joyfulness, patience, faithfulness, prayer) for His recipe for life are missing in your life? What do you need to add? What do you need more of? Allow Him to make something beautiful in you!

Lori Findlaytor

Day Sixty-One

The tongue that brings healing is a tree of life, but a deceitful tongue crushes the spirit. The tongue has the power of life and death, and those who love it will eat its fruit. Proverbs 15:4, 18:21 (NIV)

Fourth grade was a long time ago for me. About 28 years to be exact. However, I can still remember the cutting words spoken to me by a classmate. Isn't that crazy? You would think after all this time those words would be long gone from my memory. On the flip side, I still carry a note in my Bible that was written to me from a youth leader when I was in high school. Again, that was over 20 years ago!

Why do you suppose I've kept that note all these years? The answer is, those were some very touching, uplifting, and meaningful words. Every time I read it, I smile. Words, whether spoken or written, have tremendous power. King Solomon, the author of the above verses and the wisest man ever to live (other than Jesus), knew that our words matter. Our words can either crush and destroy, or they can heal and bring life. The amazing thing is, we get to choose how we use our words! The ability to communicate is an incredible gift from God. Let us then make every effort to speak words of life to everyone we encounter.

Action Over the next few days, be mindful of the words you speak. Are there more words that crush, or that give life? Ask God to help you remember the power of your words.

Nicole Byrum

Day Sixty-Two

You are of God, little children, and have overcome them, because He who is in you is greater than he who is in the world. 1 John 4:4 (NKJV)

The devil has a way of enticing us to sin. His arrows fly in the sneakiest of ways.

It's in these moments of intense war with the flesh where we need to dwell on the fact that we are more than conquerors through Jesus – He has already overcome what we are now facing and through Him, we can too.

The devil may be strong, but we have a God who has overcome the world and everything in it – that includes all the ploys of the devil – what a beautiful thought!

Next time you are tempted with sin, remember Jesus' beautiful sacrifice and how rewarding it is to resist and stay in perfect communion with our Savior.

Action Is there sin you are struggling with in your life right now? Jesus is always there and hears your every prayer. Pour out to Him what you are struggling with, ask His forgiveness, and ask Him to fill you with His strength. He will never fail you.

Olivia Bell

Day Sixty-Three

The LORD gives, and the LORD takes away. Blessed be the name of the LORD. Job 1:21 (CSB)

I remember going out one morning feeling really blessed, and I spent half my walk thanking God for all He'd blessed me with and how good I felt that day.

Do you ever get the feeling of being unbelievably happy/joyful/blessed and you wish you could feel that great forevermore, but deep down you know you won't constantly feel on a high?

Two weeks later, I walked home almost in tears. I went through a time where I was really upset and disappointed but I chose to trust that God knew best and to believe He knew what He was doing.

"Every blessing You pour out, I'll turn back to praise. When the darkness closes in, still I will say – Blessed be the Name of the Lord," (Blessed be Your Name – Matt Redman)

I acknowledge that praising God in struggles, and sticking with Him no matter the situation isn't easy – but it's important. Getting yourself to a place where you can truly worship God is so uplifting. How you get that connection and true worship experience looks different for everyone and can vary depending on how you feel. Maybe you want to dance around the room or perhaps you'd prefer to lie on the floor. You might sing out loud, or lift your arms up, or you might not.

One of the most refreshing exercises you can do is choosing to spend time in worship. Time spent in complete worship is going to enable you to withstand the storms of life.

Action Take some time today to intentionally bless the name of the Lord.

Sophie Spree

Day Sixty-Four

I have told you these things, so that in me you may have peace. In this world you will have trouble. But take heart! I have overcome the world.
John 16:33 (NIV)

We live in a troubled world.

It doesn't matter what time in history you live in, what part of the country you live in, or how much or little you own. Pain comes to everyone. It is unavoidable. But we do not have to face it alone.

Jesus told us that we would suffer. He Himself suffered while on this Earth. It is one of the consequences of sin. But Jesus tells us that we do not have to lose hope, that we do not have to fear.

"I have overcome the world." Wow. That is so powerful! Jesus has triumphed over sin and death and suffering.

We will still face trials, but we can have hope because Jesus has already won. He is victorious. And because of that, we can also have peace.

Action Take a moment to thank God for sending Jesus. Thank Him that we do not have to face trials alone. Ask Him to help you trust in Him and have peace.

Annie Joransen

Day Sixty-Five

And you grumbled in your tents and said, 'Because the LORD hates us, He has brought us out of the land of Egypt to deliver us into the hand of the Amorites to destroy us.' Deuteronomy 1:27 (NASB)

The Israelites had just crossed the Red Sea. They had witnessed one of the greatest miracles of the Bible. God had rescued them from slavery. And yet, right after, they were found "grumbling in their tents." WHAT?!?!

Why do we do that? God answers our prayers and shows Himself to us in an undeniable way and within days we're sure He's forgotten us.

This group of Israelites never got to see the Promised Land because of their continued unbelief. I don't want that for us! God has an incredible purpose for us here on earth-our Promised Land-if you will. But, we get there through our faith and obedience to Christ.

What would have happened if instead of complaining, God's people would have said, "I can't wait to see what God's going to do next!" How different their lives would have been! God wanted their complete devotion and He would have taken care of the rest. That's what He wants from us.

Action Take some time to reflect. Are you a grumbler in your faith? Or are you someone who says "Watch what God's going to do- it's going to be BIG." Start praying God would "increase your faith and help you overcome your unbelief." (Luke 17:5; Mark 9:24) Then watch Him work!

Lea Vaverchak

Day Sixty-Six

The good man brings good things out of the good stored up in his heart, and the evil man brings evil things out of the evil stored up in his heart. For out of the overflow of his heart his mouth speaks. Luke 6:45 (BSB)

If you ever want to know someone's heart, it's pretty simple—just listen to what they say. Give them time to speak. Listen attentively to them. Let them know you truly care about what they are saying. Then, as they speak, their words will inevitably reveal their heart.

Well, what if you weren't just interested in knowing only the heart of your friends and family? What if you also wanted to know the very heart of God?

The answer would be the same.

Listen to what He says. Give Him time to speak to you each day by reading His word. Be attentive to what He says. Let Him know that you truly care about what He is saying. Then, as He speaks through His word, He will surely reveal His heart to you.

Action If you don't currently read the Bible on a daily basis, set aside 15 minutes a day for the next month to do so. Pick one of the Gospels or the Psalms, and then just listen to what God has to say to you.

John Pasquet

Day Sixty-Seven

Praise be to the God and Father of our Lord Jesus Christ, who has blessed us in the heavenly realms with every spiritual blessing in Christ.
Ephesians 1:3 (NIV)

Sometimes I feel like I don't do enough. Sometimes I feel like I don't have enough. Sometimes I feel like I am not good enough. Do you ever feel that way? If you do, you are not alone!

We live in a culture that tells us we need to do more and have more to be truly happy. Just look at the movies, commercials, and media surrounding us every day. Look closely at the message they are selling.

But the Scripture tells us the truth, that God has blessed us in abundance, with every spiritual thing that we need. Jesus paid for it all on the cross, and gave us eternal access to our heavenly Father, and all His spiritual blessings…like hope, peace, provision, and joy through it all! You and I have a great and loving Father!

What is our part? What do we have to do to get these blessings? PRAISE! Praising and thanking God from your heart releases the heart of God and all His spiritual blessings in your life! You have everything that you need in the Spirit!

Action Find one thing today that God has blessed you with, and thank Him for it. Be aware of all that He has done for you, and all that He has given you. Begin to grow a heart and attitude of thankfulness for all the ways that He has blessed you!

Lori Findlaytor

Day Sixty-Eight

Though he (Jesus) was God, he did not think of equality with God as something to cling to. Instead, he gave up his divine privileges, he took the humble position of a slave and was born as a human being. When he appeared in human form, he humbled himself in obedience to God and died a criminal's death on a cross. Philippians 2:6-8 (NLT)

Do you ever wonder why we care so much that Jesus defeated death? If He's God, surely He could take the pain away and then it's not a big deal?

When I let pride or ignorance overtake me as I read the gospels, I find myself letting doubt creep in. I make Jesus' death into a small deal. It's not like He really felt it… right? Looking at this verse, I am humbled by what I read. Jesus '…was born as a human being… died a criminal's death on a cross.' He was born as a baby. He would've cried, known hunger, felt tired, and, most importantly, He experienced pain. THAT is why Jesus' death is such a sacrifice – He felt pain. He died in the same way we would've died if we had been in His place. This gives me so much hope!

When I am hurting mentally, physically, or spiritually, Jesus knows what that pain is like. He isn't sitting in the skies, keeping His distance. He lived as a human, He can empathize.

Action When you come to God in pain, know that He understands because He has been through death to save you. Let that fill you with awe as you pray.

Jessica Edwards

Day Sixty-Nine

May my prayer be set before you like incense; may the lifting up of my hands be like the evening sacrifice. Psalm 141:2 (NIV)

As I ran down familiar streets in the quiet of the morning, I enjoyed the coolness of the air and the sunshine on my face. It was a beautiful time of the day for a run. Then, the most wonderful scent of all hit me. The smell of sweet lilacs. My favorite flower. I took a deep breath in and tried to savor every second of that beautiful aroma. Instantly, I was reminded that my prayers are a pleasing fragrance to God; that my prayers to Him resemble something of the sweetness of lilacs.

In the book of Revelation, the apostle John wrote about his vision of heaven. In chapter 5 verse 8, he described golden bowls full of incense, which were the prayers of God's people. To think, our prayers are received in heaven as fragrant incense! I don't know about you, but I think that is pretty incredible! How comforting it is to know that our heavenly Father who loves us, delights in our prayers. Let us come to Him daily with our praise as well as our requests, knowing he graciously receives- and welcomes- the prayers of his children.

Action Join me in this prayer: Thank you God for not only hearing my prayers, but for delighting in them as well. Gently remind me throughout my day that you are always ready to listen. Thank you for loving me so mightily. In Jesus' name I pray, Amen.

Nicole Byrum

Day Seventy

Very early in the morning, while it was still dark, Jesus got up, left the house and went off to a solitary place, where he prayed. Mark 1:35 (NIV)

This is one of my favorite Bible verses. I realize that it seems a bit random! I am an introvert and I handle early mornings far better than I do late nights, so it could be the fact that here I can see Jesus relating to both of these, or it could be something deeper.

This verse challenges me. Jesus, who was fully God and fully man, spent time alone with God. Do I prioritize my relationship with God enough?

It gets light around 6 am in Israel. Now, I am not suggesting that you get up before six every day to spend time with God. But, what is the first app you look at on your phone in the morning? What is the first book that you read? I try and make sure the Bible app is the first thing I look at on my phone every day before I reply to late-night WhatsApps or check the weather forecast. I want to be putting God first.

Action Make a note of when you are going to spend time with God this week.

Sophie Spree

Day Seventy-One

Let us not become weary in doing good, for at the proper time we will reap a harvest if we do not give up. Galatians 6:9 (NIV)

When you are close to the actualization of your dreams, discouragement tends to set in. Those who give up can offer more than enough excuses. But our goals can only be reached if we keep pressing on.

Proverbs 24:16 says "for an upright man, after falling seven times, will get up again " This means the upright man kept trying over and over again until he made it. You are not a failure just because you failed. You are only a failure if you don't try again.

Grab any opportunity to try again. Don't sit back and self-pity yourself. Every opportunity that comes your way is for you to rise again, just as the upright man in Proverbs 24.

You have come too far to give up. Keep praying. Keep hoping. Keep trying.

Action Pick up a pen and write down 20 reasons why you shouldn't give up. Focus on the positive reasons, not the negative.

Emmanuel Olapade

Day Seventy-Two

A person's wisdom yields patience; it is to one's glory to overlook an offense. Proverbs 19:11 (NIV)

As teens growing up in this culture, some of us are extremely concerned with not hurting anyone's feelings. There are also some of us all-consumed with putting up our guard so our own feelings don't get hurt. While we can't control other people's reactions (or even overreaction), we can control ours. Even when faced with an uncomfortable situation, we always need to remember that our response is our responsibility.

All of us make mistakes, but God looks at who's first to forgive. The fact that you can forgive someone when they have done something awful to you reveals more about you than it ever will about them. Creating a habit of forgiveness is not only something God values but something that will affect you in a positive way for the rest of your life.

Action Make a list of the worst things that people have done to you, ranking them least to greatest. Ask yourself if you truly have forgiven them. If the answer is no, ask yourself and God to reveal the reason why.

Kristen McVickers

Day Seventy-Three

But you are a chosen race, a royal priesthood, a holy nation, a people for His own possession, that you may proclaim the excellencies of Him who called you out of darkness into His marvelous light. Once you were not a people, but now you are God's people; once you had not received mercy, but now you have received mercy. 1 Peter 2:9-10 (ESV)

Our identity matters.

Culture tries to tell us to find our identity in our work, our social status, our gifts and talents. These things will never bring true joy or meaning. But in Christ, we find the opposite.

God says that you are His; He claims you. He calls you His own. And because of that, our lives have purpose.

What does this passage say is our purpose? That we may proclaim His excellencies. God chose us to be ambassadors for His glory. We get the privilege of sharing who Jesus is with the world!

How can we do that? Through the way we live our lives, through the way we love one another, through the words of truth and life that we speak over others.

Action Do you believe that you are desired by God? Not just loved, but chosen by Him and given a purpose!

Annie Joransen

Day Seventy-Four

Rejoice in the Lord always. Again, I will say, rejoice! Let your gentleness be known to all men. The Lord is at hand. Philippians 4:4-5 (NKJV)

God is faithful! He cannot, and will not, ever fail you. He is trustworthy, loving, and kind. He is patient, forgiving, merciful, and so much more. Because of who He is, you can rejoice in Him! It doesn't mean that your life is perfect, or that you are always happy, but that you can celebrate His goodness! You will still have challenges and failures in life, but you can always depend on Him. That is something to rejoice in!

Because you can depend on Him, you don't have to struggle and fight the way that others do. You can have His peace deep inside you and pour it out to everyone you meet. You can show your "gentleness" as a strength to those around you. As you show your gentleness to others, it can remind you of God's great love and grace for you, and His Holy Spirit working in you and through you!

Action Ask the Lord to show you someone who needs your gentleness and kindness today. It might be as simple as a smile or a friendly hello. Allow the Lord to use you to help someone else "rejoice" in Him!

Lori Findlaytor

Day Seventy-Five

Therefore, since we are surrounded by such a great cloud of witnesses, let us throw off everything that hinders and the sin that so easily entangles, and let us run with perseverance the race marked out for us. Hebrews 12:1 (NIV)

If you've ever run a long-distance race of any kind, you may have experienced the temptation to stop running. As a longtime runner, this usually isn't a problem for me. However, there was one 26.2 mile race that was particularly grueling. I wanted to walk off the course and be done, leaving the remaining 14 miles to the other race participants. With encouragement from my husband, I kept going, persevering to the end where a race volunteer placed a finisher's medal around my sweaty neck.

You may have not known this, but God has a race marked out for you! He has gifted you in specific ways and has called you to faith for a purpose. Just think, the King of the Universe wants to use you for His glory! There will be times you may be tempted to quit your race, but God Himself promises to give the strength necessary for perseverance. And the best part? The reward for finishing our race is something so much better than any medal or trophy. I long for the day when I receive my greatest reward- to hear God say, "Welcome home, my good and faithful servant. Well done."

Action Ask God to continue to give you perseverance as you run your race! Keep a journal of the ways he has given you strength- even when you have felt tired and weak. Thank Him for His sustaining hand.

Nicole Byrum

Day Seventy-Six

Bear with each other and forgive one another if any of you has a grievance against someone. Forgive as the Lord forgave you. Colossians 3:13 (NIV)

This is not easy. Especially when someone leaves us out or says hurtful things about us to others.

I was texting a friend on social media about a light-hearted topic, but then I happened to see that I was left out of a group. I don't know whether it was intentional or not. All I know is it hurts.

I wanted to lash out, but I knew better. I wanted to retreat and hide from everyone and see if anyone actually cared about me. But pity parties don't solve anything.

But suddenly I was reminded how at one point everyone rejected Jesus. Jesus forgave me from my leaving Him out of my life, and He calls me to do the same for others.

Sometimes it looks like going and asking for forgiveness, but sometimes, in this case, it looks like surrendering it to the Lord and forgiving someone inside your heart, because they are not even aware that they hurt you.

Speaking to them later from a place of forgiveness already in your heart can go a lot further than acting out in vengeance.

Action Think of someone you need to forgive in your heart. It may not require you to talk to them. Maybe you took an action the wrong way. Create some boundaries to protect yourself, but also release yourself from the hurt this person caused by asking God to help you forgive them in your heart.

Britney Froese

Day Seventy-Seven

The heavens declare the glory of God; the skies proclaim the work of his hands. Day after day they pour forth speech; night after night they reveal knowledge. Psalm 19:1-2 (NIV)

Surely we are the part of creation that worships and obeys God the least! I don't see animals intentionally going against what God wants for them. I don't see the weather or nature sinning towards God. Creation and the natural world is still beautiful and still points towards God.

We are the pinnacle of God's creation, made in His image (Genesis 1:27). No other part of creation is made in the image of God, and none of the animals can have a relationship with Him like we can, which is unique to the human race.

Sunrises and sunsets display phenomenal colors, snowflakes are so intricate, flowers are stunning and birds sing beautifully, all these things and more can point back to Creator God.

Action Play the song 'So Will I (100 Billion X)' by Hillsong. As you listen to the lyrics that say, "If creation's made to worship, so will I ... If creation still obeys You, so will I," ask yourself: How am I worshipping God and pointing towards Him?

Sophie Spree

Day Seventy-Eight

Heaven and earth will pass away, but My words will never pass away.
Matthew 24:35 (HCSB)

A lot of people discredit the Bible because they think it seems like an outdated religious textbook that has no relevance to the current day. You may have even wondered to yourself, "Is the Bible really meant for me?"

We know that the Bible is filled with many historical details from the past. Historians have even proven its validity, as the approximate times of events in the Bible line up with approximate times of events recorded in other documents. You've probably heard the phrase, "those who fail to learn from history are doomed to repeat it". We can learn from the mistakes that the people of the Bible made, as well as follow the examples of their righteous acts.

In addition to history, you probably also know that the Bible gives us glimpses of the future. The last book, Revelation, is filled with imagery of the end times, but you'll find hints of future events sprinkled throughout the Bible. You can read a lot of prophecy in the Old Testament that didn't come to fruition until hundreds of years later in the New Testament, as well as some prophecies that have yet to be fully fulfilled.

So the Bible has both the past and the future, but what about the present? Is the Bible really alive and active in the present day? The short answer is yes! The commands and promises that God gave to people in the Bible were also meant for us and will continue to be for all people forever. I've experienced times when a Bible lesson I read was exactly what I needed in my life at that moment. If someone thinks the Word of God isn't relevant to current events, it's likely because they're not currently reading the Bible!

Action Pick a section of the Bible to read today. It could be a chapter you were already planning to read, or you could just randomly open the Bible and read the page it lands on. Even if it's something you've read before, you might get a new message from it this time around. Look for clues of the past and the future. Most importantly, look for what God wants you to read and apply now in the present.

Jessica Lippe

Day Seventy-Nine

And we know that all things work together for good to those who love God, to those who are the called according to His purpose. Romans 8:28 (NKJV)

Good things happen in life. Bad things happen in life. Happy and sad things happen in life… because that is just, well, life. You will have struggles and you will have victories. But through it all, you can have peace and joy. How? By loving God, and believing that He is working for your benefit. He is faithful and committed to you. He will never fail you!

He is always looking out for you, and even more, He is working everything out for your good. That is His promise to you. Nothing is wasted in God's purposes. Not failures or disappointments. Not shortcomings and delays. Not even mistakes and heartbreaks. He will use them all for your good… to teach you and prepare you for your best future.

Know that as a believer, you have a purpose and a destiny in God. Trust that every day, He is with you, and working all things out for your good! Because He loves you!

Action Ask the Lord to show you how He is working in a difficult situation for you. Ask Him to show you His plans and purpose for you, even in the middle of your pain. Then watch Him work on your behalf.

Lori Findlaytor

Day Eighty

See what great love the Father has lavished on us, that we should be called children of God! And that is what we are! 1 John 3:1 (NIV)

For the last year, my 11-year-old daughter has been learning French from an app called Duolingo. As I witnessed her becoming more proficient at her new language, I was inspired to brush up on my limited Spanish. Consequently, I have taken to randomly speaking words in Español around the house. A few mornings ago, as she lazily made her way down the stairs, I greeted her with, "Hola, buenos dias mi hija!" Translation: "Hello, good morning my daughter."

Now, I typically wouldn't use this style of greeting in everyday English, but the more I thought about the translation, the more beautiful it seemed. My daughter. Doesn't that sound so lovely? It's so personal, and it describes a uniquely intimate relationship.

Amazingly, the Creator of the universe- our Creator- calls us His children. Through the blood of His son, Jesus, God's love was lavished upon us. He is ours, and we are His- and nothing can ever change that! We can wake up each morning knowing God our Father delights in us. As we sleepily roll out of bed, we can imagine Him whispering to us, "Good morning my child."

Action Develop the habit of talking to God as you lay in your bed before getting up each morning. As a mom, I take great delight in my children telling me "good morning." I'm sure God feels the same- and desires to greet you too.

Nicole Byrum

Conclusion

You've reached the end of the book. But hopefully, this doesn't mean the end of your time in devotion. You've already made it nearly three months spending daily time in scripture reading, prayer, and living out your faith. Sure, it wasn't always easy, and you may have skipped a couple of days, but ultimately, you did it. Let's keep it going.

What should your day 81 look like? If there was a verse in this book that stuck out to you, why not start there? Reread it and find ways to see God's Word in a new light. Read the entire chapter it's from for context. Then keep reading until you finish that book of the Bible. Maybe you can continue reading the next book, and the next, and the next. By the time you circle back to that first verse, you'll have read the entire Bible.

Some days, you may read several chapters. Other times, you may spend days on just one verse. The amount that you read with your head isn't nearly as important as the truths that you keep in your heart. But if you'd like, you can create your own personal Bible reading plan.

Would you like another devotional to aid in your Bible reading? There are lots of great books out there you can use, but we have a few recommendations. G4C Publications released another devotional called *77 Days of Devos* by Jessica Lippe. Just like this book, the one-page devotions feature a verse and a applicable action to live out what you've learned.

If you're a girl who wants to journal during your devotional time, check out *Diary of a Girl 4 Christ*, also published by G4C Publications. This activity journal has lots of writing space to help bring you closer to Christ, including some guided writing pages to reflect on what you've read during devotions. There are also sermon notetaking pages, plus free writing and drawing pages, lists, quizzes, and so much more!

You could also consider getting a themed devotional. There are Christian devo books out there for just about any hobby or interest, including athlete and cheerleader devotionals, animal lover devotionals, and devotionals based on movies, just to name a few. The editor of this book, Jessica Lippe, wrote *Uncommon Adventures*, which is part devotional, part travel guide. The important thing is for you to find a relevant way to live out what you're learning about God. And keep learning!

Haven't found another devotional that speaks to you? Why not write one yourself? Sometimes, writing out what we've learned from the Bible in a personal way can help us understand better. If you do end up writing something, send it to us at Girlz4Christ@yahoo.com. It could appear on our blog or in our next devo book!

Do you think you're a different person than you were 80 days ago? Sure, your name probably didn't change, but other elements of your life have. It's possible that you've gone through a hardship. Or maybe you got some great news during this time. A lot of things around us can change our lifestyle, but have you changed as a person? If you've taken the scriptures you've read to heart and live out your faith, you'll likely see a personal change in positive ways, no matter what the world throws at you.

These devotions can serve as a useful tool in changing your life. Perhaps you really did experience a 180-degree change over the past 80 days. If these readings led you to start or renew your relationship with Christ, congratulations! We're excited about this 180 turn from sin and hope you continue on this new walk in life. But let's not forget what this is really all about: the one true God who never changes.

About the Authors

Annika Asplund is a twentysomething living in Ferndale, Washington. She is currently studying music at Harding University in Arkansas where she hopes to pursue a career in music therapy. Her favorite verses include Proverbs 17:17, Psalm 13, and Psalm 139:14.

Olivia Bell is a Christian in her twenties living in the mountainous desert somewhere at the bottom of the USA. She enjoys serving others, writing articles and letters, hand-lettering, drinking hot tea and collecting far too much washi tape. She is the creator and editor of Christ's Light Magazine, a free e-magazine for women, and co-founder of The Smile Project, a ministry of encouragement through the written word (both can be found on her website: Christslightmagazine.weebly.com).

Taylor Bennett is a dandelion-wishing, world-traveling lover of books, words, and stories. Her goal is to write inspiring, timeless books for girls that will touch hearts for generations to come. She loves to connect with readers on Instagram at @taylor.bennett.author.

Nicole Byrum is an independently licensed marriage and family therapist from Van Wert, Ohio. She is the author of *Remade: Living Free*, a book inspired by her work with women in recovery from substance abuse. In her free time she enjoys running, cooking, and maintaining a website which features a blog and podcast (you can check it out at nicolebyrum.com).

Tiara Cirino was born and raised in Chicago, Illinois. For fun, she plays basketball and track and field. She's been playing basketball eight years and track for three. She also enjoys cooking and being with family.

Catherine Cooley, Founder of Simply Devoted Ministry Network, is an extreme coffee lover. Being from Appalachia, she loves the beautiful outdoors. She is currently enrolled at Covenant Baptist Seminary to obtain a Masters in Systematic and Historical Theology. She is a wife, stay-at-home mom, and foster mom.

Jessica Edwards struggled with identity as a teenager and looked to the world for her assurance, before God gently guided her back to the Bible! Now she is learning day by day to trust Him and has been blessed with a godly husband and beautiful baby boy. She lives in North Wales, UK where she enjoys experimenting with new cake recipes, catching up with friends over ice cream and reviewing books for her blog, www.hurricanelove.weebly.com

Lori Findlaytor lives in Northern California where she and her husband have been married over 30 years, have 4 adult children, and 2 grandchildren. Lori is an Ordained minister, a certified professional life coach, and has recently become a certified Christian counselor. She loves to travel the world and meet new people, and bring encouragement to all those around her.

Millie Florence is the middle-grade fiction author of Honey Butter (published age 13) and Lydia Green of Mulberry Glen (published age 15). She loves sushi, zip-lines, and just about all things yellow. Find out more on her website millieflorence.com.

Britney Froese writes on her blog, britneyfroese.com, to release our insecurities, know our identity, and live out our purpose. She and her husband live in a small town in Texas. She enjoys cooking and eating pasta, reading stacks of books, and spending time with friends and family.

Kaitlyn Giesbrecht is a young teen that aspires to be a sketch artist. She lives in Saskatchewan, Canada, where she grew up with a love for dance and music. She has been dancing for 11 years, and playing piano for 6. In her free time, you can find her reading a good book or playing with her dog. Her favorite verse is Proverbs 31:25-26, because it reminds of her of who she is as a child of God.

Amber Ginter is an aspiring 24-year-old writer that currently works as an English teacher in Chillicothe, Ohio and has a passionate desire to impact the world for Jesus through her love for writing, aesthetics, health/fitness, and ministry. Hoping to become a full-time freelancer, Amber seeks to proclaim her love for Christ and the Gospel through her writing, as well as her aesthetic ministry team (Aisthitikós Joy Ministries) and various volunteer roles. She is also currently writing her first book and blogs at https://wordscanshattersilence.home.blog/.

Bethany Hamilton is a professional surfer, motivational speaker, and host of the online course, The Unstoppable Year. Learn more about her career and unstoppable passion at BethanyHamilton.com.

Nathan Johnson was born and raised the small town of Milan, Indiana. During his early teen years, after a time of lots of doubt in his faith, he spent a lot of time studying apologetics and understanding what the truth of the gospel really meant and began to make the faith his own. After a strong call to ministry during his later teen years, he decided after college to join the military to minister to soldiers and aspires to be an Army Chaplain one day.

Annie Joransen grew up in the Midwest, but now resides in Atlanta, Georgia, with her husband. She is a teacher-gone-entrepreneur who believes that learning is a gift and should be fun! In her free time, she enjoys hand lettering, being outside, and creating resources to encourage others in their walk with the Lord. You can follow her at annie.joransen on Instagram for biblical encouragement and tips for intentional living.

Jessica Lippe is the editor of this book as well as a contributing writer. In addition to running Girlz 4 Christ, Jessica has written several books, including *Uncommon Adventures*, *77 Days of Devos*, and *The Ultimate Survival Guide to Working at Camp*. She loves bargain hunting, travel, and adventure, which she documents at JessicaLippe.com.

Kristen McVickers lives in a small town in North Carolina. Playing volleyball and talking are her comfort zones, however, she has been known to write on occasion. Even though she's just 16 and a junior in high school, she has plans to attend college to become a PTA (Physical Therapist Assistant).

Becca Nicholson, part of the sister-duo The Sonflowerz, has been recording music, writing and traveling for 15 years. When not on the road, Becca can be found enjoying the Rocky Mountains with her husband Bryan and daughter Lily. Her favorite things are chocolate, British tea and showing her daughter how to garden. Her book, written with her sister Elissa, is titled Made to Shine: A Girls-Only Devotional, now available everywhere. Connect with Becca on her socials (Instagram @Sonflowerz) or at www.Sonflowerz.com.

Emmanuel Olapade is the CEO of Nuel Foods, a brand that specializes in processing and packaging food with excellence. He is also the author of Seed Of Life Devotional, a devotional that spreads the words of hope and good news to a dying generation. He writes spirit-filled and life-changing articles while living in Nigeria.

John Pasquet was deeply influenced by the Navigator ministry in college and later served for two years in Ukraine with Campus Crusade for Christ. He now works as a computer programmer in Columbia, Missouri, but his greatest joy is opening the Scriptures with international students and scholars through his involvement in a local ministry.

Sarah Susanna Rhomberg is a reader, writer and herbal-tea-lover who lives in Europe. At a young age she said "yes" to God and has never regretted her decision. Sarah lives her life for Christ and writes to glorify Him.

Sophie Spree is blessed to live in a particularly beautiful part of North Wales, in the UK. The twenty-year-old recently spent six months on a Youth for Christ gap year doing youth work, media and communications, and is now waiting to see what God has for her next! She likes reading, writing, video editing, and walking. She enjoys the odd bit of table tennis and, random fact, doesn't like honey!
https://www.youtube.com/watch?v=IBF0TXbE3WY

Hahnna Tokich is a 24-year-old artist who lives in the Pacific Northwest with her husband Jarad. Her favorite color is cotton-candy pink (and you can't convince her otherwise). She dreams of being a Mama one day but for now fills her apartment with all the plants she can get her hands on.

Hannah Udobia is a lover of Jesus and a former student of The Writers Bureau, Manchester. She has been published in Independent Australia, Relate Magazine, The Teen Magazine, and Ruby Plus Africa Teen Magazine.

Lea Vaverchak resides in Martinsburg, WV with her husband, John, of ten years and two young children. She is a former elementary school teacher and currently a freelance writer for David C. Cook ministries. She is the founder of Girls For God and hopes to expand the group in the years to come, so girls everywhere are able to join. Her website is www.girlsforgod-gfg.com.

Talia Ward was born and raised on the Oregon Coast. For years, she's been passionate about encouraging others in their relationship with God through her writing. In her free time, she loves singing, art, and spending time with her husband, Austin.

About G4C Publications

G4C Publications seeks to provide quality Christian media for girls (and guys) around the world.

Their previous books include:
Girls Who Change the World
77 Days of Devos
Diary of a Girl 4 Christ

G4C books can be found on Amazon in both Kindle and paperback, or ordered at your local bookstore. Visit their website at Girlz4Christ.org.

Read more books from
GIRLZ 4 CHRIST
publications

 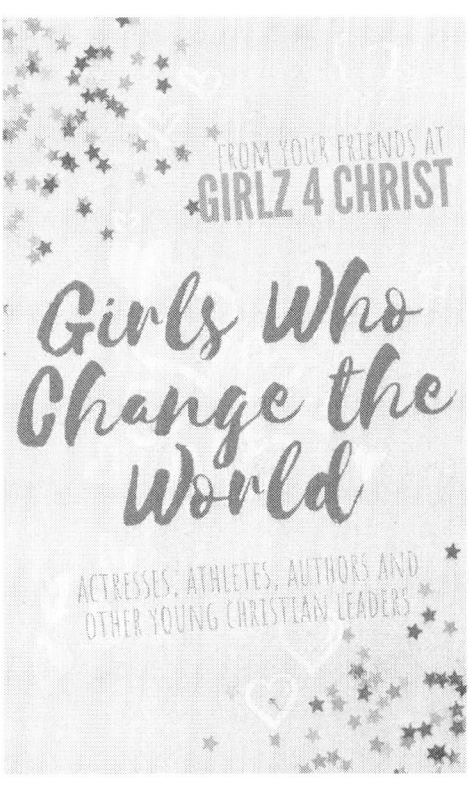

Find out more at *Girlz4Christ.org*

Printed in Poland
by Amazon Fulfillment
Poland Sp. z o.o., Wrocław